1983

University of St. Francis
GEN   371.102 H862
Howie, Patricia Anzalone,
Behavior modification :

P9-AQQ-492

BEHAVIOR MODIFICATION:

A PRACTICAL GUIDE
FOR THE CLASSROOM TEACHER

Behavior Modification:
A Practical Guide
for the Classroom Teacher

Patricia Anzalone Howie
Gretchen Winkleman

LIBRARY
College of St. Francis
JOLIET, ILL.

Parker Publishing Company, Inc.   West Nyack, New York

© 1977, by

PARKER PUBLISHING COMPANY, INC.
West Nyack, N.Y.

*All rights reserved. No part of this book
may be reproduced in any form or by any
means, without permission in writing from
the publisher.*

Library of Congress Cataloging in Publication Data

Howie, Patricia Anzalone,
    Behavior modification.

    Includes index.
    1. Classroom management. 2. Behavior
modification. I. Winkleman, Gretchen,
joint author. II. Title.
LB3013.H68   372.1'1'02   76-27718
ISBN 0-13-072678-8

Printed in the United States of America

371.102
H862

105,197

To the eight most important children in our lives,

Austin
Charlie
Diane
Mark
Patricia
Tamara
Valerie
Warren

Also by the author:

Individualized Teaching in the Elementary Schools, by Dona K. Stahl and Patricia Anzalone. Parker Publishing Company, Inc., 1970.

HOW THIS BOOK WILL HELP
THE CLASSROOM TEACHER

The dynamic principles of behavior modification can make every teacher's job more stimulating and rewarding. The major purpose of this book is to provide practical guidelines and specific know-how to translate tested approaches into action—quickly and easily.

Although the concepts and practices of behavior modification can be applied in many settings with individuals of many different ages, the effective programs and techniques described here will have special appeal for you, the elementary classroom teacher. It is you who "lives" within those four walls with Norine while she cries all day long. It is you who watches David wander around the room until you think you are ready for the nearest padded cell. And day after day and week after week it is you who faces the frustration of seemingly unavailable specialists and recommendations that are often impractical for *your* situation. No one has to write a report to tell you Jeff has a problem; what you need is reliable help—*fast,* both for the child's good and your own.

This book will enable you to begin analyzing and changing procedures almost immediately. The first part will acquaint you with some basic terminology. How old is behavior modification?

What did Pavlov and Skinner contribute? And what *is* behavior modification anyway? What do terms like *inhibition* and *operant conditioning* have to do with your Monday-Tuesday-Wednesday world?

Since you must start with yourself if you are to be a "behavior modifier," the next section of the book deals with key aspects of your own role. What is the structure of behavior patterns you have already set up in your classroom, knowingly or unknowingly? Are you encouraging behaviors you would really like to eliminate? What specific changes could you make *tomorrow* in the way you arrange your furniture and use materials already available? What inexpensive commercial materials will help you strengthen this approach? How can you reorganize the materials you have to fit in with your new goals?

With this group approach as background you will be ready to deal effectively with the behavior of individual children who need special attention. In the next portion of the book you will find practical techniques for coping with a number of common behavior patterns. Which approach is best for a disruptive child? What can you do to help a withdrawn child? How can you use existing resources most effectively? How can you analyze and overcome such problems when there is no school psychologist or counselor available?

The last part of this book provides answers to important questions currently being asked about the use of behavior modification in today's schools. How can you use such methods in situations other than the self-contained classroom? How can you use specialists without depending upon them too much? How can your principal help? How can you help parents change from being part of the problem to becoming part of the solution? And should you ever admit that the problem you face is beyond your ability to solve within the classroom?

As you read, jot down comments that come to mind, especially names of children with whom particular ideas might help. Start trying things just as soon as you can, and note the results. Techniques described will be appropriate for rural, suburban or urban schools; and most are workable without waiting and without monetary cost.

When you acquire the ability to modify behavior and *maintain* the change, you will make a priceless contribution to learning and to the happiness of your children . . . and to yourself.

Patricia Anzalone Howie
Gretchen Winkleman

Acknowledgement

People write books because they think they have something to say. This effort is no exception. We have tried to use our backgrounds and experiences to communicate material we consider helpful. Only the reader can judge whether or not we have succeeded.

We have enjoyed working together; we suspect you would have enjoyed sitting in on some of our writing sessions!

Many have helped us, especially Miss Frances Woods, Mrs. Hilda von Goehde, Dr. Sidney Koret and Dr. Gerald Winkleman. Our families deserve special thanks, for their forbearance (which we have tried to reward) and their advice (some of which we appreciated).

P.A.H.
G.W.

TABLE OF CONTENTS

13

1 GETTING A REALISTIC VIEW OF BEHAVIOR MODIFICATION

"I've had it," shouted the fifth grade teacher, as he slammed down his luncheon tray. "That Alice talked all morning long, and the others didn't get a thing done."

"If only they would put Earl into a special class where he *should* be, I could really *teach* for a change," said another.

"I want to resign—I know I am not in control of that classroom," said a third professional to his building principal.

Sound familiar? These comments and many more like them are being voiced by classroom teachers everywhere. Perhaps you have said, or thought, something on this order yourself at one time or another.

Oh, how you would like a fairy godmother to come into that classroom and perform some plain everyday miracles! If only she could get that one student into a special class. If only there could be enough psychological testing, done the day you ask, with reports back in twenty-four hours. If only she could arrange it so those special-area people would be available when you want them. Oh, and while we're at it, if only you had a decent room, with the space to separate some of the problem children from one another.

But there is no fairy godmother; there will be no miracles. You will probably have the same group for the rest of the year, except for a few students whose families move in or out of the district. Getting a place for a child in a special class will not be any easier in the future than it was in the past. Psychological testing and reporting will presumably continue at the present frustrating speed. And it is not likely that you will be provided with an all-new, fabulously modern classroom before June.

So *face the facts:* if changes are going to "happen" in your classroom this year, *you* are apparently going to be the one to *make* them happen. Are you willing? Will you risk changing "the way I've always done it"? If so, you're on your way.

The rest of this chapter will give you background you will need. Perhaps it does not matter where ideas came from, as long as we have them now and they work. If this is your philosophy you may want to skip the next few pages—temporarily or permanently. If, however, you feel that knowing the background of a tool like behavior modification (or behavior therapy, as it is sometimes known) would give added understanding in your use of it, read on.…

PRACTICAL LESSONS FROM FREUD AND PAVLOV

Since ancient times man has sought to control his environment, including the people around him. For centuries fathers have been giving sons carpentry tools or musical instruments, hoping that they would like and use them later in life. In the oldest of schools, teachers were praising and punishing. In prisons, criminals were punished by isolation and torture, but rewarded with early release for "good behavior," so that these wrongdoers would associate the punishment with the crime and stop breaking the laws. Mental patients have been restrained or physically abused, at least partly so that this would influence their future behavior. There have even been learned men who thought that punishment of illness would help in some way to prevent its recurrence.

These are all illustrations of man's attempt to control the behavior of others. So, you see, the concept of changing behavior is not a new idea at all. It started long ago and continues into the present, whether or not anyone analyzed the techniques or gave them fancy names.

But let's go back a bit to the late 1800's, when psychological research was changing from philosophical to practical by means of more controlled scientific experimentation. Freud and his followers placed primary emphasis upon a person's inner feelings, regarding bizarre behavior as the symptom that indicated something was wrong. At the same time other psychologists such as Pavlov were focussing upon the importance of the symptomatic behavior itself.

Freud believed that you exhibit certain abnormal behavior because you have many internal fears and anxieties which influence your functioning as a human personality. Everyone has such fears, he said, but if these are so strong that they interfere with daily life, one needs professional help. It was—and is—often a lengthy process to find out which anxiety is causing the problem. You must look into the dim and distant past with the help of a highly-trained psychiatrist or psychoanalyst. Only then can you understand the hidden reasons for your actions.

Once you have revealed and examined these inner emotions, you are ready to build an emotionally healthy outlook which will by itself produce appropriate behavior in you and enable you to function properly in society. If, on the other hand, appropriate behavior does not result, Freudian psychologists would say that you are showing *outwardly* (by your symptom, your behavior) that you still have a problem *inwardly*. Then you must again search your past with your psychiatrist, to find another past crisis which might be causing the trouble.

Sechenov, Pavlov and others believed that what has happened in the past or what is happening deep down inside you right now does not matter. The important point is that you are behaving in such a way now that you are causing problems for yourself and/or someone else. It is the undesirable behavior that needs analysis and change.

Although there had been philosophers and scientists before him who sought to explain normal and abnormal personality in terms of behavior, Sechenov did significant work in Russia during the latter part of the nineteenth century. Evidently he was quite a colorful figure, a scientist-philosopher who became the center of much debate during his lifetime. To many he was controversial as a philosopher because of his materialistic approach to life, but people came to hear him because of his study of natural reflexes and inhibitions in animals.

THE CONDITIONING PROCESS

Before going any farther, let's take a closer look at the conditioning process itself. What is a stimulus? Could you explain a *response* or an *inhibition* to someone else right now? If not, here is some material to help you with the basics.

> A *stimulus* is something in the environment which produces a change in the behavior of an animal or person.

In laboratory experiments it might be a buzzer or a flashing light; in everyday life it might be the sight of a particular person or the sound of a certain song.

> A *response* is the particular behavior or pattern of behaviors which is changed because of the stimulus.

If you faint at the sight of blood, the blood is the *stimulus* and your fainting is the *response*.

> *Conditioning* is the conscious or unconscious association of two stimuli, so that they are closely related to one another in the learner's mind.

Since snow falls when the weather is cold, we have been *conditioned* to expect the weather to be cold if we look out the window and see snow.

> An *inhibition* is the decline in reflex strength due to the introduction of a second stimulus.

If a child is approached by a dog (first stimulus) the child might pet him (response) and with this experience repeated become *conditioned* to liking and petting dogs. But if a dog that he pets should nip him or knock him down (second stimulus), he will become *inhibited* to a greater or lesser degree. This particular child will pet dogs a bit more hesitantly in the future, or else, in the case of a strong *inhibition,* he may try to avoid dogs altogether, as well as anything that reminds him of dogs.

UNDERSTANDING THE CONDITIONAL RESPONSE

Sechenov's application of his philosophical beliefs in actual laboratory observation was historic. But many consider his profound influence upon his fellow countryman, Ivan Pavlov, to be his greatest accomplishment. Pavlov carried on a great deal of well-organized research, mostly on the concept of "conditional response." He considered responses he induced to be temporary, *conditional* upon the stimulus. (In the years since his work the term "conditioned response" has unfortunately been substituted, leading to the impression that Pavlov considered such reactions fixed, mechanical and somewhat permanent, not his intent at all.)

Pavlov found that he could form conditional *reflexes* in dogs, and then eliminate or change them.

> A *reflex* is a predictable stimulus-response behavior.

This manipulation of the behavior of laboratory animals was significant, because he found he could induce various neuroses in his dogs almost at will. All he had to do under his controlled conditions was to vary the ways in which he presented the stimuli. Then he found he could reverse certain behavior patterns by creating emotional stress. The fact that not all dogs reacted the same led him to broaden his studies to allow for "individual differences." When Pavlov found many basic behavioral patterns of his dogs remarkably parallel to those of human society, he began to realize the practical implications for treatment of human behavioral disorders.

In the years that followed, much research was carried on by both psychotherapists and behaviorists. Since both Freud and Pavlov were basically concerned with correcting human behavior by modifying the responses of the central nervous system, it should come as no shock that research following both philosophies developed along lines quite parallel to one another.

BEYOND THE LAB

The usefulness of Pavlov's work was magnified by B. F. Skinner, who sought to establish the difference between *respondent* and *operant* conditioning.

> *Respondent* conditioning is conditioning in which the situation is under the control of the *experimenter*.

He presses a button releasing food according to any desired schedule, for example.

> *Operant* conditioning is conditioning in which the situation is under the control of the *subject*.

Skinner used apparatus in which the rat could press a bar himself and receive food. In this latter case the rat could condition himself and operate somewhat beyond the complete control of the experimenter.

It was the concept of operant conditioning which took conditioning beyond the walls of the laboratory, because it opened up the possibility of using a person's environment and the person himself to help correct his own *maladaptive behavior patterns*.

> *Maladaptive behavior patterns* are sets of behavior which show the individual is not adjusting well to his environment.

105, 197

LIBRARY
College of St. Francis
JOLIET, ILL.

Yet during the late thirties and early forties it does not seem that much was done to apply this research among people who needed it. In Russia there was a continuation of experimentation with animals in laboratories. In the U.S. this was a period of theorizing and academic debate.

The end of World War II changed all of this. With the readjustment to a peacetime economy there arose a monumental demand for psychological help. The wartime wife had missed her serviceman-husband; she took a job—often in a defense plant—and grew to enjoy the satisfaction of independence. Now she was forced to adjust back to the role of submissive housewife, while her globetrotting, veteran-husband coped with problems of schooling or occupational uncertainties. At this time the general public was starting to assume more of its rightful responsibility for the emotionally-disturbed. People were seeking psychological help and asking questions about their personal problems; most had difficulties for which a lengthy and costly psychoanalysis was neither suitable nor available.

As a result, interest in behavior therapy grew considerably during the forties and fifties. There were theories, studies and clinical projects in many different directions. Some sought to formulate terminology more acceptable to all experimental psychologists. Others tried to apply findings and methods to the clinical and "real world" settings. Still others began to apply the behavioral approach to the theory of learning and the field of education, although most research on this remained within the realm of experimentation. In these fields and many more there were those who were always ready to give simplistic behavioral answers to complicated psychological questions; although considered naive by fellow psychologists, they provided enthusiasm for the behaviorist movement because of their obvious confidence in its approach and application.

Thus the behaviorist movement continued to mature in the sixties. Although psychoanalysis continued to treat many individuals, psychological clinicians frequently began to combine their conventional psychotherapeutic techniques with those of behavior therapy, using what they thought was the best of both worlds with varying emphasis. Increasingly, both philosophies seemed to admit that they needed one another. Thus they were led to a greatly increased impact upon the whole field of psychology, as well as on education and society at large.

Although it sounds as if a great deal of investigation has taken place during the years since Sechenov and Pavlov, behavioral psychology is still a comparatively young field of research. The seventies have seen a continuation of exploration and refinement. Concepts of the behavioral approach have now been applied in many areas of life, at least on an experimental basis. Use of psychologists in public schools has greatly increased, leading to a current movement of *directive teaching* and whole programs of behavior modification of groups.

Directive teaching is the arranging of the learning environment for maximum usefulness to each learner.

Widespread use of commercial kits and learning systems were a natural outgrowth of directive teaching and the individualized approach currently popular in the American classroom. (This whole topic will be discussed more fully in Chapter 6: "Assigning Tasks to Produce Behaviorial Change.")

In recent years, as counselors and psychologists were added to the staffs of many districts and individual schools, classroom teachers were thrilled. Now they would have someone with both expertise and time to help them cope with behavior (or "discipline") problems in their classes. It was inevitable that many classroom teachers would develop an unrealistic idea of what that counselor would be able to do in the time he had available. The seeming inaccessibility of these specialists has proven to be just as much of a frustration to psychologists and counselors themselves as to the classroom teachers they seek to serve.

Meanwhile two types of problems have been developing in classrooms in regard to children with maladaptive behavior patterns. Some such children pass from classroom to classroom, largely unnoticed and untreated. Others are treated incorrectly, with different—often worse—behavior patterns formed, reinforced and established by teachers who know somehow that *something* needs to be done. All of this seems to flourish beyond the scope of influence of district specialists whom most teachers seldom see.

Programs of behavior modification have become recognized as a way for such specialists to extend themselves and make more effective use of their time. Many techniques and materials can be used successfully by a classroom teacher; this has appeared to be a big selling point for using behavior modification to solve the whole time problem. Thus a counselor can help more teachers by serving as a resource person to them, allowing them to run their own programs and adapt them according to their own needs. Properly run, such programs and methods can help treat maladaptive behavior patterns now untreated or treated inappropriately.

Behavioral concepts have been applied to an increasing extent in business and industry. Programs of incentive and reward, basically behavioral management, have been found highly valuable. High morale and increased production mean bigger profits for everyone!

Meanwhile, on the current scene, psychotherapy has been making its own contributions, dealing with peoples' problems through use of its own methods. But because behavior therapy is adaptable to treatment of groups as well as individuals, it has gained great popularity. Psychotherapy, with its individual orientation, seems to be more operative in psychiatric clinics and the private practices of psychiatrists and psychoanalysts.

In recent times there has been, in our opinion, a horrendous abuse of some behavioral techniques. Classroom teachers should not be using the same approach as is appropriate for clinicians. Some methods being used currently by clinicians seem to be of doubtful value, even with seriously disturbed children. You should not, for example, spend your day doling out candies to a child, while constantly trying to explain to the others why they cannot have any. You should not ever feel you are sitting in front of your class like a scientist watching rats in a box, pressing buttons or running activities by a time-clock. Distribution of worthless plastic toys to children who perform like circus animals has no place in a *good* program of behavior modification. And you should not feel it is necessary to spend evening after evening reading records and making plans for some big, splashy, merit-type demonstration of your professional wizardry.

Furthermore, programs of behavior modification are not wedded to any particular philosophy. Because in the past many behaviorists have been animalistic or mechanistic, it is often assumed that one must be similarly persuaded to use behaviorist techniques and profit from research in this field. This is simply not valid. Just as an astronomer sees order in the universe and uses it to study the heavens and to predict celestial happenings, so also the "behavior modifier" can appreciate the principles by which human learning takes place and use them to advantage.

SUMMARY

Behavior modification is the changing of another person's behavior to help him adapt more satisfactorily to his environment. Although behaviorist psychology has, through the years, developed upon a philosophy far distant from that of psychotherapy, the two have moved ever closer together, especially during the last decade. Use of operant conditioning in schools is now growing because it can be applied by classroom teachers in group settings, as well as by clinicians in individual settings.

2 CLARIFYING KEY FACTORS THAT AFFECT BEHAVIOR

Living with a classroom full of children for five or six hours each day can be a taxing job. When everything goes as hoped for and children eagerly attend, participate, share and grow, teaching is one of the most rewarding of all professions. At the other extreme, hours of teacher planning and effort may yield apathetic, frustrated, "acting-out" behavior in a few children; this truly destroys the learning environment for the rest of the class.

Where can a teacher go for help when children experience difficulty in learning and, therefore, behave inappropriately and generally change what should be a professionally rewarding job into a minute-to-minute battle for control? Most schools have some professional human resources available: fellow teachers, supervisors, school psychologists and resource teachers. Ultimately, though, real change in any teaching-learning environment rests with the individual teacher assigned to that classroom.

In-service training and experience itself develop a teacher's repertoire of skills to deal effectively with most children most of the time. But this process can take years. Most experienced teachers look back upon their first few years of teaching nostalgically, but with wonderment that both they and the children survived. Occasionally the new teacher does not survive professionally and leaves the field during or following his first year.

Consider the fragmentation of your own pre-professional training. The discipline of education was probably broken down into somewhat discrete morsels of content and theory called courses. But your experience was unusual if your schooling provided you with a central focus for these many separate pieces of knowledge. Then suddenly it was time for student-teaching, and you were expected to integrate your educational knowledge while applying it, a difficult if not impossible task.

The remainder of this chapter will show why and how behavior modification can be this integrating factor.

BEHAVIORISM

A behaviorist looks at an individual's observable patterns of life adjustment and concludes that this total set of behaviors has been learned. He does not deny the existence of instincts and drives but assumes them to be components of all individuals, as are arms, legs and stomachs. How then does he account for the great differences among people as seen in their behavior?

For the answer to this we must look at the basic needs of all people. The behaviorist believes that we all have remarkably similar fundamental requirements, nurturance (here meaning visible, physical needs of food, shelter and clothing) and security (here meaning unseen intellectual, emotional and spiritual needs). In an effort to meet each of these we behave in a certain way. If we meet that particular need by that behavior, we will repeat the behavior whenever we have that specific need. If a baby cries and receives food, he will cry the next time he needs food.

As time passes and similar situations continue to arise in an individual's life, he practices what he has previously learned and is rewarded, ignored or punished accordingly. Thus he develops his own unique system of *coping skills*.

> *Coping skills* are behaviors a person has learned to use in meeting his needs and in overcoming any barriers to meeting these needs.

Ideally the individual will develop coping skills that meet his needs in ways that are appropriate to his environment and the expectations of others around him (adaptive); unfortunately he may also develop one or more coping skills that are inappropriate to or even destructive of his surroundings (maladaptive. These maladaptive coping skills not only fail to help the individual, but may also destroy his chances of making a satisfactory adjustment in society.

THE CASE OF JEANNE

The following case history will serve to clarify the difference between a behavioristic and a more analytical (Freudian) study of one child's behavior. Jeanne was a physically beautiful girl of twelve when first referred to the mental health team at Alexandria School. When I first met her she was standing outside my office, waiting for me to administer the first of a series of psychological tests to her; I would have judged her to be sixteen or seventeen.

Until recently Jeanne's school work had been outstanding, including gifted art work and creative writing; these had endeared her to her teachers for several years. Her referring symptoms now were a sudden and total disinterest in academic achievement, along with an almost total devotion of time and effort to flirting with or annoying the boys in her sixth grade class. She had also become very belligerent toward her teacher, Miss Smith, and spent much time with Mr. Keys, the assistant principal, who frequently acted as counselor for children experiencing difficulty. She was constantly causing great commotion in the girls' locker room, which was usually unsupervised by the male teacher. Although Mr. King (the physical education teacher) had seen some of the pugnacity, he felt he could control her.

Many hours of individually interviewing and testing were followed by case-conferencing with school personnel, specialists and Jeanne's mother. All of this yielded the following explanation of Jeanne's newly displayed, maladaptive behavior patterns. Jeanne's mother, a beautiful woman, had a history of many complicated love affairs following her divorce from Jeanne's father. Two years ago, when Jeanne was ten, her mother became convinced that all men were potentially dangerous, and that economic and emotional survival—for a female—depended on the sexual manipulation of these powerful and dangerous male beings.

It became apparent that much of Jeanne's art and creative writing work had grown increasingly precocious during the last year, or since about age eleven. Outstanding nude drawings and themes of "love," "lovers" and "love unrequited" replaced former childlike themes. Jeanne, however, continued to earn and receive the verbal praise, high grades and other forms of encouragement she had come to expect.

During this time she expanded her use of sexual themes. Continued trouble with Miss Smith meant more time in counselling with Mr. Keys, sessions filled with Jeanne's accounts of her mother's latest adventures, real and imagined.

Mr. King had said he could 'handle' her, but further investigation of this revealed that this meant actual *physical* handling: he would put his hand on her shoulder and physically restrain her whenever she had launched an attack on male or female peers. Mr. King felt this physical reassurance should have been sufficiently helpful to control Jeanne and to ensure her containment afterwards in the halls and regular classroom.

Analytically—yes, Jeanne was an emergent adolescent. She may have had unresolved Oedipal conflicts or ego deficiencies not resolved during her latency years. Her mother's problems and irrational solutions acted as a behavior model for Jeanne as she attempted to grow into adolescence toward womanhood. *Behaviorally*, however, she was being rewarded for maladaptive behavior regularly at school. She was commended for producing nude drawings and love stories, and she was learning (with the help of concerned and well-meaning adults) that all of her mother's inappropriate coping skills do have a payoff. "Sass the weak female (Miss Smith) and you get the strong, reinforcing counselor (Mr. Keys)." "Attack the weak peer females in the locker room and you get the physical reassurance and reinforcement of the strong physical education teacher (Mr. King)."

JEANNE'S PROGRAM

Actual treatment of Jeanne was a long and arduous procedure, involving the efforts of many people. While her mother's more complex problems were being solved, Jeanne was placed in a foster home and behavior therapy was begun. When she was able to maintain herself in Miss Smith's room for two hours, she earned one half-hour to help Mr. Keys with his routine office work. She was allowed to do his filing, answer his phone and help catalog his personal library. Appropriate behavior for the physical education problem consisted of dressing for class in the Health Office, until adults responsible for her, and Jeanne herself, felt she could handle the locker room situation. She was transferred to a class with a female teacher, and was allowed to "earn" time to serve as that teacher's aide in classes with younger learning-disabled children.

Note that understanding Jeanne's problems and how best to help her required an eclectic diagnostic work-up: that is, a combination of the two approaches described (analytical and behavioristic) with actual treatment following behavioristic lines. Knowing when, how and why the maladaptive coping skills developed was necessary in order to consider Jeanne an individual with unique background experiences (the analytical or historical aspect). Then an effective program was used to stop rewarding her for inappropriate behavior and start rewarding her for appropriate behavior.

Productive programs to alter behavior patterns are individualized. Logically, this individualizing process begins with an assessment of the individual's present needs, but to both analyst and behaviorist this means collecting pertinent data about the person's difficulties, past and present. The analyst would study the learner's past experiences to expose the fears and anxieties which he feels need to be faced and overcome. The behaviorist would study the person's past experiences to identify past (pre-existent) influential stimulus-response (SR) sequences which presumably have encouraged the development of certain maladaptive coping skills. He would also evaluate the present (existent) SR sequences, to discover which stimuli are evoking which responses to maintain or expand these inappropriate behaviors. (Programs meant to alter behavior which lack this concern for pre-existent factors are mere gimmicks, without scientific or professional basis; some we have seen approach quackery.)

Jeanne's case was severe. As we have said, it required an extensive case history and work-up. Most of the problems with which you will be dealing will require far less background analysis, but you must seek information available on the children you teach, especially those with any serious learning problem.

THE TEACHING-LEARNING FOCUS

Many educators seem to view teaching as "something that teachers do," whether or not learning occurs. "I taught those kids long division last week. Why don't they remember any of it?" a teacher may moan, as if his presentation of the subject automatically assures that the class learned everything he presented. We would do well to use the word "present" in such a context, rather than "teach."

When we say we "present" a lesson, we are saying nothing about the reaction of others to our presentation, only that we gave out some information. "Teaching," on the other hand, refers to the presentation of certain concepts plus the learning of these same concepts by an individual or a group. This is an important distinction. Learning is taking place all the time, everywhere. While that long division lesson was being *presented,* Mary Lou learned the long division, so we can say that the teacher *taught* Mary Lou some long division. But Valerie and Tammy may have learned to wiggle their noses at one another during the same lesson time. So for them, the teacher was *presenting* a lesson on long division. They were learning, but not the concepts presented.

THE CASE OF MARIE

The following case history will illustrate this behaviorist concept, that a true "teaching" or "instructional" activity must result in learning the concepts presented. Otherwise we cannot say that any "instruction" or "teaching" occurred.

Marie, a university senior, began her student-teaching experience by observing an astute master teacher. On this particular day the entire first grade class was to have its regular math lesson. Years of experience had equipped the teacher with many pedagogical techniques which had every child eagerly attending and participating. Every conceivable approach was employed, including manipulatives, overhead transparencies and even a rhythmic activity in which children arranged themselves in sets and subsets. Marie was overwhelmed by all this, and legitimately impressed. This was the kind of role for which Marie had trained; now she saw that teaching could be exciting and learning could be fun.

At lunch Marie verbally applauded her master teacher, but was puzzled by the reply. "I do this each semester for each student teacher, to prove a point," was her sponsor's comment. "There can be a whole lot of what some call 'teaching' going on, without children learning much."

"What do you mean? Are you suggesting that those children weren't learning anything?"

"Well, perhaps it isn't fair to say that they weren't learning *anything*. They may have learned that school can be fun or that I am a nice person. And, of course, it is important for them to like school and me. But basically I was supposed to be teaching them to do that page on sets and subsets in their workbooks. When we go back to the room I'll show you what I mean."

That afternoon she gave out the math workbooks and asked the children to do a page covering the same concepts as the morning's lesson. The children were instructed to work the page independently. Marie observed that three children finished the work successfully in a few minutes. Another ten struggled along and, with the teacher's help, completed the work in about twenty minutes. The rest of the class began with the group but soon lost interest for one reason or another; they displayed various behaviors indicating frustration and tension. These seemed relieved when the work period was over and the workbooks were collected. A quick appraisal of the class's work revealed what the master teacher already knew, that less than a third of the children could really apply the concepts presented so cleverly less than an hour before.

Marie was fortunate; throughout her student-teaching experience she was given many opportunities to develop this awareness of her role in the teaching-learning process. Many of her fellow students never had such an enlightenment; they began their careers assuming that superior teaching (which would be superior "presenting" in our context) would always result in the intended learning. Marie knows better, that real teaching will produce real learning, and real learning will be reflected in behavior. As teacher she can observe this behavior and conclude that the child or the class now knows whatever-it-is.

Far too many teachers make this mistake, presenting lesson after lesson, and then blaming the children for failing to learn. Only when it is obvious that the whole class is totally confused does the teacher look for another approach, another mode of presentation, a new textbook. Report cards are often issued with comments like these:

"John could do better if he tried."
"Irma tries hard to do the work, but will not attempt new work without my assistance."
"Marco has a short attention span."

These may be saying, in effect, "I did the teaching; it's his fault if he didn't do the learning." More harmful yet are teachers' comments following an unproductive review:

"We've been doing this for days. You ought to know it by now."
"I just explained that; weren't you listening?"

These remarks reflect the real teaching-presenting focus of many practicing educators.

A good teacher would also look at another important aspect of the learning situation, one referred to earlier in this chapter:

children may not learn what is being presented, but instead they may learn subtly destructive behaviors and attitudes.

The following are some attitudes frequently taught in such situations (there are many more):

1. My failure to learn in exactly the manner expected by the teacher means that I (child) am stupid.

2. My failure to learn is my (child's) problem, not the teacher's.

3. My failure to learn means that I (child) am less than acceptable to the teacher.

4. My failure to learn is a sign of my (child's) defectiveness, which I must hide at all costs.

As you can see, some of the most vital learnings which take place in your classroom may never appear as objectives in your plan book. You teach the children how to feel about themselves, their school, indeed about society itself. These learnings may be positive or negative, but you may be sure they are always there, in one form or another. As unstated objectives (or "non-objectives," as we might call them) they are learned through systems of response and reinforcement we unknowingly set up and operate within our classrooms every day we teach. Figure 1 illustrates this: certain behaviors might reveal that the desired learning is taking place, but care must be taken to avoid the assumption that concepts or attitudes beyond those observed have been learned.

WHERE DOES LEARNING OCCUR?

Before children enter school they learn informally many skills considered essential for success in the formalized educational setting. These learnings result largely from the child's trial-and-error attempts to meet his various needs. Every child requires nurturance plus approval, attention and love. During these early years his language develops enough for him to communicate these needs to others, so that they can supply what is needed. As a result the quality of language may vary greatly from child to child. If the mother is overly involved with her own

If you want a child to...	His behavior could be...	You could not assume...
know the letters of the alphabet.	1. singing the alphabet song. 2. naming the letters as you flipped cards out of sequence. 3. writing letters that you named.	1. anything else except that he knew a song. 2. that he could write them without cues. 3. that he associated sounds with letters.
develop his interest in science.	1. reading books on scientific topics. 2. doing the experiments suggested in the science books and explaining his results. 3. writing answers to test questions in science.	1. that he could transfer the information he recalled to a practical situation. 2. that he could evolve and test his own hypothesis. 3. either of the above.
respect the rights and privileges of others.	1. telling you how children should behave toward one another. 2. attending lectures and movies on successful interpersonal relationships.	1. that he would when not observed by an adult authority figure treat anyone honestly or respectfully. 2. he heard or saw the content being presented.
enjoy good literature.	1. reading stories assigned by you and answering questions about plot, style, characterization, etc. 2. to stop relating information about "low" quality literature.	1. that he would ever freely choose to read this type of story without direction. 2. that he had abandoned "low" quality selections, only that he could discriminate who not to talk to about these selections.

Figure 1

survival, language development may be retarded. She may have ill health, overwhelming housework demands, too many children to care for properly, or any one of the myriad of other problems which minimize her ability to attend to this particular child. If, on the other hand, the mother is overly attentive to the child, he may continue to point at something he wants, rather than talking to name the object. He received a *payoff* (food or toy, for examples) without having to speak at all, so there is no reason to communicate further.

Observation of any class of young children reveals great diversity in behavior because of this diversity of language development in their early years. When their behaviors in school are what the teacher expects, things go well. The teacher responds with a payoff (smile, verbal praise, etc.) and the child is said to have made a "good adjustment to school." But when some children must learn new techniques for wants-needs gratification, then the teacher will not respond with a payoff as often, and the child is described as immature or making a "slow adjustment to the school situation." And when still others, like the child of the overwhelmed mother described above, enter the classroom, they encounter serious problems. They have learned to meet their needs by physical force or some other behavior which is now counter to those associated with success in this new situation. These children will need to change their whole repertoire of behavior patterns if they are to become acceptable to their peers and teachers.

For some this adjustment never does come to pass. School becomes a mysterious place where the rules are different. The techniques that worked for the child at home no longer pay off. In his confusion he begins to accept negative feedback in preference to no attention at all. Unless this pattern is reversed there will be trouble for all three: parent, teacher and child.

Essentially, then, children need to have at their disposal techniques which will enable them to manipulate others to meet their basic needs in a socially acceptable manner. Most educators dislike the use of the term "manipulate," but recognition of the child's active part in the learning process will help us to gain more appropriate and productive control. We must not let children do as they please. On the contrary, *we must reward them only for the type of behavior that will lead to the learnings we wish them to absorb.* We need to concentrate on this all day everyday, complimenting those who follow directions, those who do their papers on time, or those who produce creative science projects. *On the other hand, we need to start ignoring some of the minor "misbehaving" when no one is being hurt physically and no property is being damaged.*

One of the dividends of such an approach is that the student will soon learn to understand the principles of cause-and-effect in behavior, a concept he can then use in the rest of his world. If both teacher and child understand and use guidelines set within the classroom framework, it should be easy for most children to apply this same machinery to life beyond the school.

WHOM ARE WE TEACHING?

Education as a discipline relies heavily upon the methods and products of other disciplines. Psychology contributes much to our knowledge of individual children and how they learn. Sociology has shown us that ours is a pluralistic society with many cultures and subcultures. The crosscurrents, especially between societal elements, are at once sources of strength and conflict. No one can deal effectively with an individual's behavior without having some notion of the societal groups which engendered that child.

The children we teach are simultaneously unique individuals and group members with much in common. Because of this, formal education for any child should build upon his psychological (individual) and subcultural (sociological) background, and incorporate both accurately into his schooling. Education becomes an immoral enterprise whenever it takes as its aim the development of homogeneity. Programs for behavior modification must combine accurate knowledge of the child's uniqueness with an acknowledgement of his need to grow in his own real community. Without this basis the thrust of behaviorism becomes another misapplied technology in education.

HOW CAN WE CHANGE BEHAVIOR?

Prior events have shaped the child's behavioral patterns, and there is really nothing that you can do to change history, but altering present and future patterns of experience and payoff is possible. It is downright essential if you are to guide children toward responsible autonomy.

We must assume that children are most homogeneous in readiness for learning at birth, and that from this point onward they become more heterogeneous. This is due to two factors: the uniqueness of the individual organism to receive and process stimuli in given experiences and the diversity of experiences available to process. Therefore at all educational levels, but especially as the child enters school, his individual readiness for new learning must be assessed. Stated curriculums and generalized assumptions must give way to a realistic view of the individuals you are hoping to involve in the learning process.

We have already established that each child enters school with his own set of coping skills, based upon his own individual set of experiences. Now we must decide which coping patterns we will accept and develop, and which we should reject and change. Planning for individual learning sequences means first determining long-range goals for each child, by considering what behavior patterns will serve him best in the years to come. (Teachers often assume that patterns set in the classroom are also those which will be useful and acceptable at home and in future experiences; this is not always so.) Only then can we decide our long-range "destination" for an individual, what set of behavior patterns we picture as being most useful to him as he grows up.

If a certain profile of behaviors is the "destination," then the next step must be to set short-range goals to provide guidance along the way. And indeed it is a process much like planning a trip: pinpoint on a map where you are now, where you are going, and then what places you must pass through to get there. These short-range goals (or sub-goals) will help both teacher and learner to reach long-range goals by a positive pathway.

THE CASE OF MARTHA

In changing any child's behavior, it is' vital for you to identify the stimulus that preceded any unwanted behavior. The case of Martha illustrates this point and shows how you as a classroom teacher can help.

A small and frightened seven-year-old, Martha always became frustrated and tore up her paper minutes after she had begun working. Then she would put her head down on her desk. If her teacher tried to talk to her, she was apt to cry and bolt from the room. Martha was soon known as the class "baby" and "dummy," a position her steadily deteriorating behavior earned for her. Midway through the school year she was referred to the school psychologist; the teacher wanted an assessment of this minimally-functioning and immature child.

A complete examination by Martha's family doctor showed she was in good health; results of thorough vision and hearing tests were within normal ranges. Individual psychometric evaluation revealed that Martha had superior ability in all but one subskill area tested: her ability to understand and execute auditory directions. More specifically, her auditory memory and sequencing skills were severely impaired.

In discussing Martha's behavior, her teacher agreed that she had no trouble with written tests or directions in any subject, nor did she ever become upset when working on individual projects or in informal learning situations. Even during her most difficult days she seemed to function acceptably much of the time. Only when her work assignment required following long and involved verbal explanations and directions did she exhibit behaviors that were disruptive and self-defeating.

If her teacher had accurately analyzed the situations (stimuli) which preceded Martha's undesirable behaviors, formal diagnostic testing might have been unnecessary. Psychometric data are useful in confirming the dynamics of behavior and in gearing instructional strategies to the learner's capacities. But to be most useful, data gleaned from formal evaluative procedures must be combined with anecdotal records of observed behavior. (See Chapter 12 for more detailed help on recording behavioral observations.)

Structuring a program of behavior modification for Martha involved minimizing the lengthy verbal instructions which triggered the unwanted behavior, while complimenting her when she did follow directions correctly. Her new instructional program was the same in subject matter that it had been before; directions became written as often as possible, and oral directions—when necessary—became a series of short directions, dividing complex tasks into many simpler and smaller ones.

Her limited auditory ability was no longer the factor on which her classroom success depended. As a result Martha was able to function satisfactorily.

WHICH SKILLS OR CONCEPTS SHOULD WE TEACH?

It is the task of formalized educational systems to advance the learner toward actualizing the potential which is uniquely his own. Each year brings changes in the body of knowledge he is expected to learn, with yesterday's impossibilities becoming today's scientific discovery or political reality. Change itself becomes the one reality of which we can be sure. Educating for an ever changing world requires the development of tool-skills in learners, not the assimilation of facts soon to be outdated.

This shift from acquisition of facts to development of skills poses another problem for educatiors: it is relatively easy to evaluate whether or not the learner has memorized a given fact, but relatively difficult to evaluate whether or not he is acquiring some abstractions and attitudes, such as perceiving reality or formulating appropriate goals.

Educators in areas of curriculum are helping to define that basic body of knowledge a person will need and use in today's world. Focus on *content* and *information-likely-to-change* must be replaced by developing *the ability to cope with change itself.*

WHEN ARE BEHAVIOR MODIFICATION TECHNIQUES MOST EFFECTIVE?

Many years back a group of teachers was asked which grade level was the most important; they quickly answered, "First grade!" They went on to say that this was the point at which the foundation learnings occurred. If the child was unready for formal instruction during this first year, the foundation would be unsteady and each year would surely see these unready children falling farther and farther behind.

Educational realities also tell us that if John did not learn the reading skills last year in first grade, I as the second grade teacher might suspect that the first grade teacher was remiss in her duties. In a similar chain the first grade teacher may wonder about the work of the kindergarten teacher, and kindergarten teacher about the child's early training at home by Mother and Dad.

Each totally misses the point; that is, what might be done in the present. Each grade is the most important grade; each day is the most important day, for both child and teacher. *Today* the child needs a positive learning experience, and it must be planned with full awareness of his readiness. The teacher is responsible for utilizing all professional tools at his command: knowledge of developmental psychology, psychometric test results, ability to diagnose educational needs and the perception to translate the learner's exhibited overt behavior each day into rationally conceived educational objectives.

SUMMARY

Today's educator must function as a highly skilled professional, capable of determining appropriate learning sequences for individual children. The development of these professional skills is a continuous process of observing the behavior of children and assimilating knowledge from contributing disciplines such as psychology and sociology. The ability to interpret behavior diagnostically and to change educational objectives into stated behavioral sequences toward stated behavioral goals is the first half of being an effective teacher. The second half is the ability to analyze and restructure reward systems which develop and maintain learning.

When goals are rationally conceived and the learner is rewarded extrinsically—and eventually intrinsically—behavior will change. Increasingly, children will become responsible for their own behavior.

3 ANALYZING YOUR PRESENT REWARD SYSTEMS

It is a humbling but reassuring reality that we are all greatly influenced by the *SR* sequences in our lives. We would like to feel that we are the "captains of our fate," but unfortunately we live in a real world where we do not have complete control over the people and things around us that influence us from day to day and from year to year. Marie, the student teacher referred to in the previous chapter, became the kind of teacher she was influenced to be, for example. The reassuring part of all this is that we are able to analyze our own behavior and make changes in ourselves that will greatly improve our relationships with students and fellow teachers.

Recently the mother of a bride-to-be gave her daughter a manual on how to train a dog. Needless to say, the girl was puzzled. "What is this for?" she inquired.

"Take my word for it," answered her mother, "treat your husband according to the same principles and you will have a happy marriage." The implied parallel was upsetting but also intriguing. What could training a dog have to do with her beloved and their coming marriage?

Out of curiosity she started reading the book one evening. She found that what the author was suggesting was to reward appropriate behavior and ignore—or try to ignore—any inappropriate behavior. Sensing a great measure of wisdom in her mother's gift, she tried to analyze the principles she read about and apply them to the marriage relationship. The results you may already have guessed: the marriage was an extremely happy one, relatively free of the nagging and other negative aspects of such an adjustment. When he was on time for dinner, for example, she rewarded him with a smile, a pretty dress and dinner by candlelight; when he was late without calling she gave him the same food, but with fewer of the "trimmings"—and no negative remarks. In reality this bride was structuring a system of rewards. In doing so she became a positive thinking, perceptive young woman with an adoring husband and a happy home.

Human relationships are basic to both marriage and classroom. As teacher, you have just as much responsibility for your classroom and its atmosphere as our friend the bride did for her marriage. As leader of your children, you have both the right and the moral obligation to plan, structure and modify any and all rewards and reward systems in your room.

A good, hard look into your personal teaching mirror is a constructive—and often brave—step toward improving the learning climate of your classroom and the reward systems operating there. Look at your own responses to the ways your children act and "produce." Look at the rewards children give one another, such as the sense of power the class bully receives from cowering classmates. Perhaps without realizing it you are encouraging such behaviors when you really want to eliminate them.

This chapter will guide you through an analysis of your own classroom reward systems. It will also suggest many ways in which you can use your leadership to improve these systems by applying the principles and procedures of behavior modification in the learning situation.

WHAT IS A REWARD? WHAT IS A REINFORCER?

Let's go back to the SR sequences of the children themselves to investigate this matter of rewards. Take a good look at Stuart. Here are just a few of his behaviors, along with the response each evoked:

Stimulus Behavior	*Response Behavior*
making funny faces	reprimand from teacher, snickers from friends.
quiet work	no visible reaction from anyone.
pushing people in line	sent to princìpal's office for lecture.

Without knowing anything more about Stuart, which behavior(s) do you think he would repeat? Why?

You're right if you think he would repeat the funny faces and the pushing, for that is just what he did. His home offered neither affection nor recognition. He needed to have someone notice him. When he worked quietly in class no one noticed or recognized him, but if he made faces or pushed people around he got attention immediately.

Stuart considered it important to get attention, so to him it was a *reward* when the teacher or the principal scolded him.

> A *reward* is any visible reaction that a person considers important.

Furthermore, Stuart's frequent use of the SR sequences noted above *reinforced* his maladaptive behaviors.

> *Reinforcement* is the repetition of the same reward for the same behavior.

When a behavior is reinforced it continues and grows stronger; when a behavior is not reinforced it weakens and disappears.

To help Stuart his teacher might try a behavior modification program something like this:

Stimulus Behavior	*Response Behavior*
making funny faces	teacher will ignore.
quiet work	teacher will praise Stuart for time he works quietly, at first for three minutes at a time, then longer. She will also reward him by allowing him to be leader of the class line to lunch when he meets the standards set.
pushing in line	as leader of the line, he should have recognition and less need to push others; teacher will ignore occasional instances of pushing.

In this program the teacher's verbal praise acts as a *positive reinforcer*.

A *positive reinforcer* is one which acts as a stimulus to the individual, so that he is stimulated to repeat the desired behavior.

The teacher's commendations for quiet work give Stuart the attention he craves while stimulating him to repeat the "quiet work" behavior.

A *negative reinforcer* is one whose *removal* acts as a stimulus for the individual to repeat the *desired* behavior.

(Mild electric shock used for bedwetters is a widely-known example.) If Stuart's teacher detains him until the others have gone to lunch, this might be a negative reinforcer and eliminate his "pushing" behavior, but only if it makes Stuart want to go to lunch with his friends enough to make him behave appropriately; thus he would receive the reward of rejoining his class in the lunch line. In this illustration Stuart may possibly interpret the detaining as a payoff, in that he is receiving attention from the teacher in the process. If this happens he may repeat the pushing in order to repeat the teacher's response of attention. This would change the negative reinforcer (detaining) to a positive reinforcer (attention) and the pushing behavior will be reinforced, not eliminated.

In some behavior modification programs it is considered appropriate to use candies and other "tokens" as reinforcers. It is our opinion that such rewards are unnecessary and even harmful, especially when used in the classroom. A smile or a star on a chart will accomplish just as much. Even in the treatment of children with severe behavioral disorders, any use of nurturance materials invites confusion in the child's perception of either teacher or parental roles, or both. We recommend avoiding the use of tokens altogether in the regular classroom and very cautious use of them elsewhere.

THE PROOF IS IN THE PAYOFF

A payoff is really what makes a behavior continue. Many times, without realizing it, we respond to children in ways they perceive as payoffs. Here are a few commonly-used responses. Which have you used most frequently?

- grades
- comments with grades
- rubber stamp for outstanding work
- praise in note to parents or on report card
- allowing the class to play a game during free time
- stars on a chart
- your reading a story to the class

- choosing a well-behaved student to run an errand
- your smile

You may have used several or all of the above to reward individual students or the class for behavior you considered appropriate. Now look at this second list. Do any of these look familiar?

- scolding a child for sharpening pencil at the wrong time
- your dirty look
- tearing up someone's paper in public
- sending someone to the principal's office
- making someone apologize
- yelling, privately to individual or publicly to class
- lecture on how you expect more from students this age

Yes, these are also ways in which you (and we) have responded to students. *These are payoffs for certain kinds of behavior.*

Now here is a third list, with some responses you may not have classified as payoffs before:

- your physical nearness to a child
- kissing or hugging a child who cries
- slamming a book down on your desk
- sending the class late to physical education class or lunch
- placing a child's desk near yours
- embarrassing a child
- verbal threats: what you will do if the room is this noisy again, etc. etc.
- keeping a child in the classroom while the rest of the class goes to some other activity

As you can see, you are rewarding all your children constantly, in these ways and many more. Reinforcers come in all shapes and sizes and are not always received by the child the way you meant them to be received.

To apply this, try listing the five or six worst behaviors shown repeatedly by your students. Choose things that really annoy you, such as writing on the furniture, fighting when you were out of the room, swearing or shuffling noisily down the hall. Then beside each behavior note the way you respond when students act this way. What payoff do you give? Did your action deter the child or the group from repeating that behavior? Why not? Perhaps you gave them a payoff which became a reinforcer, so that they were encouraged to repeat the behavior. In many cases, of course, this was the opposite of what you intended.

WHAT IS SUCCESS?

Some children never seem to be able to stimulate the teacher to respond with a positive reinforcer for constructive achievement. The child is dirty or unable to follow directions. For some reason he can seldom produce papers worthy of a star. So he resorts to behavior that will at least give him some attention and fill an emotional need. He seeks *some* kind of payoff, even if negative. To these children any response equals success: they are able to get a payoff. And so they repeat the pattern, continually reinforcing their own behaviors.

Most children who do acceptable or outstanding work receive some kind of positive reinforcement from the teacher, often enough to encourage their repetition of the success-producing behaviors. But even these students are not immune to problems; if they do not continue to receive sufficient praise and recognition they too may resort to the attention-getting devices and negative payoffs. It is so easy to assume that these students will go right on doing their work well while you pay attention to those who "need help." And so in an effort to meet his emotional needs such a student may suddenly exhibit anti-social behaviors or inferior work you will *notice*. At this point he probably feels (consciously or subconsciously) that your expression of disapproval is to be preferred to no notice at all. To him right now, this is success.

Somehow, then, you need to supply each individual student with success. To some this may only mean a word of encouragement from time to time, or an assignment that obviously credits him with superior ability. To others it may be a very short and simple assignment a child can complete on his own. Maladaptive behavior is a danger signal that should tell you that somehow this child or this group needs a payoff not now being supplied.

TEACHERS NEED PAYOFFS, TOO

Yes, children are not the only ones who need to have their behavior reinforced. Teachers need success, attention and the same satisfaction in their own worth. What payoffs do you value most as a teacher? Do any of the following stimulate you to do your best teaching?

- praise from the principal (private)
- praise from the principal (public)
- praise from other teachers
- smiles of students
- smiles of *certain* students
- a quiet room
- high scores on district or state-wide tests
- your paycheck
- being able to leave the building at proper dismissal time
- having students who are reluctant to go on to the next activity

Most of us would quickly agree that we do have needs to meet. But we must also face the fact that we have the authority to give our own goals and feelings priority over those of the students. Consequently we are in a rather dangerous position, for we can, for example, insist on the room being quiet because we need it that way, while our students may have a need almost the opposite, the need to work together in groups and learn from each other. But since we teachers are more powerful, we can impose our wills upon the class. We may even boast that "in my room my word is law." Yet even in such rooms as this there are students maneuvering to manipulate the teacher, prodding with certain behaviors they know are unacceptable, until we break down and supply the payoff scolding.

DO NOT DISTURB

We have encouraged you to try out any of the techniques mentioned in the early part of this book, so that you would become acquainted with the everyday possibilities of behavior modification in your classroom. Now it is time for you to take the first major step toward implementing these techniques with a *program* involving you and your whole classroom. This involves the payoffs you yourself work for in your teaching. Do you think you have good goals, in all honesty? What kind of payoff should be important to a "good" teacher? Are these important to you?

How willing are you to change what *you* have felt you needed, if you could know the learning atmosphere in your room would improve? What degree of quiet would you absolutely have to have in order to function? What kind of reactions from your students would—or should—please you most at the end of the day? ...at the end of the year? Are you willing to put aside your "Do Not Disturb" sign for one that says "Construction Ahead?"

Modifying your own goals and needs to include those of your students is not as difficult as it may sound. Suppose you realize that you yourself need a fairly quiet room at certain times. There is nothing wrong with this. But surely the room need not be sepulchral all day long. And when you need a more subdued atmosphere, you need not wait until it is noisy and then yell to the class that you can't stand it that noisy. How about trying to notice and praise when the class is functioning at a lower noise level? Perhaps before you start the next class you could say, "My, I was just noticing how nicely you did your independent reading assignments." Then, when the class does get noisy you could give them directions for the next lesson and begin almost immediately with those who heard and are ready to work. They will feel rewarded, and the rest will probably follow along when they can see there is no payoff scolding in sight.

Observe yourself constantly. As you spot and analyze deviant behavior in your children, check that you are not reinforcing and maintaining it yourself. Leave a tape recorder running during the most difficult part of the day; it will help you become more aware of your own behavior patterns and how they contribute to your classroom atmosphere.

SUMMARY

As teachers, we have the authority but not the right to impose our wills upon the children we teach. Since we are responsible for the learning that takes place, we must become very observant, continually changing the way we deal with children when it needs changing. Our task as teachers is to show the child by our reward systems what we think is important. If we give priority to his needs and reward behaviors that lead to learning, we will experience success and personal growth.

4 STRUCTURING A PROGRAM OF BEHAVIOR MODIFICATION IN SELF-CONTAINED CLASSROOMS

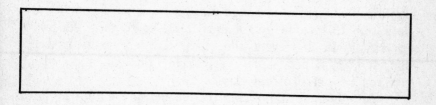

The self-contained classroom usually consists of one teacher and a group of children numbering about thirty. Class begins at nine o'clock and dismisses at three. With the exception of a fixed lunch-time, the day's schedule is under the teacher's control. All subjects are taught in the same room in a true self-contained classroom, although many schools have extended the definition to include use of music, art or physical education specialists. In any event the classroom teacher is basically considered the person responsible for the education of all children assigned to that class.

To fully understand what the teacher of the self-contained classroom is dealing with, we must first realize the importance of the concept of *significant others*.

Significant others are those persons who interact with an individual frequently, and whose ideas or actions are considered important by that individual, either consciously or subconsciously.

These are the human influences acting constantly upon all people everywhere. To the housewife, the soap opera star may be a *significant other*. To the hermit, the characters in his books may fill this role. But in an educational setting the significant others usually consist of other children and teachers fitting the definition.

62

SPECIAL CONSIDERATIONS FOR SELF-CONTAINED SETTINGS

The influence of significant others in the self-contained classroom needs to be examined in order for a teacher to use it best in that setting. Here is a summary of more crucial advantages and disadvantages.

Strength	*Weakness*
1. Teacher highly-motivated, since she planned the program and set the goals	1. Limited support of fellow-teachers due to their lack of involvement in program
2. Limited number of human relationships to manage within the four walls	2. Solutions limited to resources in the one room
3. Expectations clear and stable—set by one person	3. No one to identify any inconsistent or unworkable expectations except teacher herself
4. Person interpreting data (as program evolves) also has authority to alter patterns of contingencies	4. Teamwork, consultation and other advantages of the group process impossible
5. Freedom to develop an appropriate program for group or individuals in it	5. Easy to forget that desired objectives take time and that new patterns of pupil behavior evolve rather than erupt

The following case history illustrates the way one teacher used some of the strengths of her self-contained situation to modify the behavior of one child.

THE CASE OF HELEN

Helen was a very large and withdrawn girl. Her interactions with peers were characterized by sullen or snarling nonverbal responses. When provoked about her failure to participate in any school task Helen was apt to attack her provoker physically.

Because she upset the class frequently, she was difficult—if not impossible—to teach. Her teacher tried to maintain enough calm for Helen and the rest of the class to function. When Helen grunted, grimaced or yelled, "He's picking on me," her teacher would answer her with low-keyed calming words of comfort and encouragement. In spite of this, Helen invested no time or effort in her school work.

Miss Northrup, Helen's teacher, was aware of Helen's background and her early childhood, which can only be described as "deprived." Because of her inability to deal with others, Helen was disliked by the other children since she first started in public school. So Miss Northrup, an empathetic and concerned teacher, tried in every way she knew to give Helen some of the love and support which was so painfully lacking. Yet each of Helen's interactions with her peers continued to reinforce Helen's feeling that she was in fact an obnoxious person, unworthy and unloved.

In discussing Helen's case with a psychology professor at her graduate school, Miss Northrup expressed a desire to initiate a program that would change some of Helen's behaviors. The professor agreed, and the program was set up as a course project.

As they discussed Helen's background and the strange behavior she was exhibiting, Miss Northrup described the way in which she related to Helen in various situations during the school day. As an infant Helen had not learned socially acceptable ways of gaining attention and recognition, so she developed inappropriate techniques for doing it. Her maladaptive behavior continued in Miss Northrup's room as she received attention she needed by causing classroom commotions and arousing the sympathy of her teacher.

Psychologist and teacher decided that first of all Miss Northrup was to attend carefully to all of Helen's interactions with others in the room. She needed to activate a basic principle of behavior modification in classroom settings: *The first person who must change behaviorally is the teacher.* What was it she was doing to maintain Helen at this regressed and unsocialized level of development? Miss Northrup kept a simple anecdotal record of daily classroom happenings to find out. She left a tape recorder running as much as possible and tabulated the information on a chart like this:

Helen to Miss N.	Miss N. to Helen	Helen to Classmates	Classmates to Helen

By means of the tapes, the chart and her own impressions, Miss Northrup was able to determine that she was indeed encouraging Helen to remain a sullen, uninvolved girl. When Helen withdrew and looked sad or forlorn, her teacher reached out to her verbally or physically. When Helen became negatively involved with her classmates, Miss Northrup interceded; by supporting Helen she reinforced Helen's feeling that she could not support herself.

Again Miss Northrup conferred with her professor. What should she do? He suggested two teacher behaviors she should change:

1. Each time Helen was part of a classroom disruption, Miss Northrup was to ignore her and deal only with her peers.

2. Only when Helen's behavior approached a socially acceptable standard was her teacher to recognize her presence.
   (Both of these took supreme effort on the part of such a warm and concerned professional as Miss Northrup.)

They also discussed possible tasks that might be assigned to Helen. They must be activities that she enjoyed and that were within her capabilities. These would provide something positive for Helen through which she could achieve recognition from Miss Northrup.

Each morning for the first week of the behavior modification program, Helen was assigned to listen with headphones to a tape of three currently popular songs. Her follow-up assignment was to discuss with her teacher which of the songs she liked best and why. There was a lot going for this assignment:

1. The activity was known to be a favorite.
2. She was capable of using the tape recorder.
3. The headphones would eliminate possible distractions.
4. Positive teacher-pupil interaction was structured into the activity.
5. Classmates could complete their own assignments undisturbed and (hopefully) improve their opinion of Helen.

During the program, all negative behavior was to be ignored as much as possible. When Helen withdrew from group activities, Miss Northrup was not to speak warmly to her as before. By agreement with the school principal, the office waiting area was chosen as a place where Helen could be asked to stay when her behavior could no longer be ignored in her classroom. (This was treated in a matter-of-fact manner, not as a punishment.)

While ignoring negative behavior, Miss Northrup was to respond positively when Helen was able to communicate with words rather than grunts and groans. By responding to Helen she would communicate to Helen that this was a behavior she wished Helen to continue.

The first morning of the program Helen arrived with her clothing in the usual state of disrepair. She approached her teacher with a nudge and a grunt, obviously wanting her to pin the front of her blouse where two buttons were missing. Miss

Northrup ignored her altogether, because this was unacceptable behavior.

Helen dropped her head and came closer. "I think you're trying to tell me something, but I'll wait for you to tell me in words," said Miss Northrup.

Although Helen continued various nonverbal attempts to gain the usual mothering attention, these were ignored. And so it went throughout the first week.

By the second week Helen could not tolerate being ignored by her teacher. In desperation one morning she blurted out, "Fix my bow!" Although this was rough, at least it was a beginning. Helen was talking.

Progress in the taped assignments followed the same slow pattern. At first Helen thought the teacher was rejecting her when she isolated her with the headphones. Then she went through a stage when she would listen to the music but fail to report back to the teacher, for fear she would again be ignored. Miss Northrup did not remind her continually of her responsibility; she simply repeated the assignment each morning and let it go at that. It was some weeks before Helen could consistently complete this simple assignment on a regular basis.

Eventually this program of behavior modification worked for Helen. In the three years since then she has become a receptive child who utilizes a few peer relationships quite well. Although she has not become a scholar in any sense of the word, she can follow simple assignments in the classroom and rarely disturbs others as they work. Recently she has begun to see herself as really capable of learning; she applies herself to a daily tutoring session with a high school volunteer.

There are many Helens and many Miss Northrups, too. The program described is a comparatively simple one, which most teachers could carry out successfully. Such programs of behavior modification, however simple, are possible and necessary in self-contained settings with minimal support for the teacher. Could Miss Northrup have done what she did without the help of her professor? Most assuredly she could have, with equal effectiveness.

QUESTIONS TO ASK YOURSELF

1. Do you believe that children must be considered as individuals, with programs differentiated to meet their individual needs?

   If you do, then it will not strike you as unfair to single out one child for "preferential treatment," be it exceptional reward or the withholding of something that that child values.

   We do not expect children to look alike or dress alike. If children wear different size shoes, grow at varying rates or prefer different foods, we accept these differences. It is equally important to accept the principle that each child requires differentiated educational planning and treatment if our efforts are to have relevance for that child's life.

2. Do you want the child to change?

   Miss Northrup wanted to "give" to Helen. Despite the child's self-defeating behavior patterns, her teacher had not realized that by accepting and excusing Helen's behavior she was limiting the child's opportunities to grow experientially. It was difficult for this kind teacher to follow the program and ignore a child so needy of friendship and approval. But once Miss Northrup had decided that she had to behave in a relatively "unkind" way in order to help Helen change inappropriate patterns of behavior, she gritted her teeth and acted upon what she knew was best.

3. What are you doing that makes the desired change impossible?

   The child came to you having mislearned. You inherited the problem, in most cases, rather than causing it yourself. But you also have a personality and "automatic" reactions that cause you to deal with certain children in certain ways. Do you have the fortitude to listen to and tabulate your own tapes, for example?

Whether you will simply live with an uncomfortable situation and enjoy complaining about it or determine to analyze and correct it is a choice only you as teacher can make.

4. What is it the child can already do?

If your program of behavior modification is to get off the ground successfully, it must offer opportunity for the child to receive some positive reinforcement immediately. Chapter 3 discussed the concept of rewards and reinforcers. To apply this concept you must identify some area of *relative strength* in the child and build upon that. (Miss Northrup knew that Helen could not read, write or participate in classroom discussions, so she did not assign her to do any of these at first. Helen had few academic strengths, but she *could* listen to music. This was for Helen an area of strength on which to build.)

Each child can do *something* well:

He may not be ready to . . .	But he might be ready to . . .
. . . read a book	. . . find all the pictures which interest him.
. . . solve a page of math problems	. . . look at newspaper ads to find the range of prices on used Fords
. . . work alone for thirty minutes	. . . work alone for three, five, or six minutes
. . . tolerate a classroom discussion	. . . listen to a tape with material about the topic being discussed by the class
. . . work in a subgroup of six or seven children	. . . work with one other child.

5. Is equal treatment your goal?

How do you explain to the other members of a class why one child is receiving a different type of treatment?

If you have satisfied yourself that programs for children must be differentiated and that this particular program is right for this particular child, you will not have any trouble communicating this to your class.

Children accept the fact of human differences and will accept the fact of differentiated programs as long as the teacher communicates that this is the procedure he will follow. The children will accept what you are doing for another child when they are secure in their own unique relationships with you as teacher. It is only when children are insecure in their relationship with a teacher that they begin to compete for attention and favors.

SUMMARY

The self-contained classroom offers few support systems to the teacher. In spite of this limit it is altogether possible that he can initiate and run a program of behavior modification in a way that will be effective. Although there is a lack of resource personnel to help diagnose and encourage the teacher in such a setting, this can work to his advantage, in that it is a more controlled situation with fewer human relationships to worry about.

By analyzing ways in which he is maintaining maladaptive behavior in his pupils, the "behavior modifier" can easily initiate successful programs to change reinforcements and behavior patterns. An improved learning atmosphere will be the result.

5 ARRANGING YOUR ROOM TO PRODUCE BEHAVIORAL CHANGE

```
┌─────────────────────────────────────────────┐
│                                               │
│                                               │
│                                               │
│                                               │
└─────────────────────────────────────────────┘
```

A classroom is an environment. We cannot call it "natural," like the wooded glen with tadpoles and fronds of fiddlehead fern; we could not even call it "real," like the angry blacktop world where the inner city child learns to survive. On the contrary, classrooms are highly controlled settings, and may also be described most of the time as artificial. The factor of control is important, because it means we are able to create within the classroom almost any kind of framework we want for our instructional programs.

The type of setting we wish to structure is not limited by the age or architecture of the building. Even experienced educators expect to find old programs in old buildings and new programs in new; but this does not have to be the case at all. Some time-worn structures house programs that encourage children to live, learn and relate well to others, and there are ultra modern architectural showplaces that inhibit learning and discourage children from developing responsible autonomous behavior.

More important than the age or location of a school building are the nonverbal messages sent out constantly from its walls and windows. School districts struggle continually with the effects of old and new school buildings upon the staffs within them. Teachers in older buildings are often jealous of those in newer schools, even though both may receive equal supplies and other resources.

In the same way, classrooms communicate to the students who come to them what will be expected of them during their time there. Of course there are architectural features of a classroom that cannot be changed; but most of the signals sent

72

out by a classroom can be changed to solve many problems voiced repeatedly by classroom teachers.

In viewing the classroom as an educational greenhouse, most teachers would want it to say things like this:

1. I (the classroom speaking!) separate children from the confusion of overwhelming stimuli available outside.
2. I help the teacher to focus the childrens' attention upon details they might otherwise miss.
3. I hold a protected world, where children can concentrate on testing their ideas with a minimum of distraction.
4. I provide a place for examining elements of the "real" world in greater detail.
5. I am a place where the teacher can meet the needs of individual children through differentiated expectations and materials.

If we are not careful, however, we may hear the classroom saying things like the following:

1. I am a place where children are forced to do things that have little or no meaning to them.
2. I help separate the children from meaningful experiences abundantly available outside my walls.
3. I help the teacher create an artificial world, real within itself but unrelated to the childrens' real world.
4. I provide a place that is confusing and contradictory to children.

Most of the messages sent out from classrooms are non-verbal, encouraging behaviors and evolving values without your ever saying or doing anything as a teacher. This chapter will help you design the kind of classroom setting that encourages those learnings that you value.

A HORRIBLE EXAMPLE

Not long ago we were allowed to visit an experimental program for children with behavioral and emotional problems.

This was a governmentally-funded program, housed in one of the larger midwest universities.

The room was large, airy and completely carpeted. The diagram below shows the general layout of the wall with large windows, the two walls of mirrors and the row of study carrels. Furniture was new and colorful. The two mirrored walls and the window wall were all covered with construction paper from the floor up beyond a child's eye level. There was no visible sign of either school supplies or childrens' work. As we began our observation the seven children were seated as shown. The teacher was seated with them.

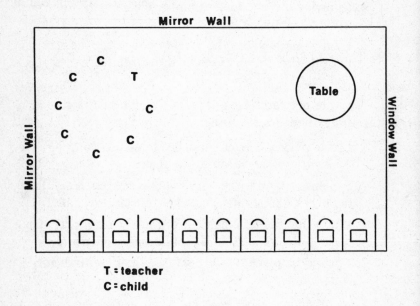

T = teacher
C = child

Her appearance attracted our attention immediately. She was an attractive young blonde teacher. But from a belt around her hips hung seven kitchen timers, each a different color. Her wrist was braceleted with a roll of wide masking tape. As the lesson began, we watched and listened intently.

The teacher was presenting a lesson on initial consonant sounds. As we watched, most children followed the first part of the lesson, listening politely and responding when called upon. But after about eight minutes she asked the children for "a word beginning like 'bird' and 'boy.' "

Without being called upon one boy emerged from a robot-like trance and began to tell an anecdote about his pet bird. Without a word the teacher stood up, tore a piece of masking tape from her "bracelet" and placed it on the boy's mouth. Then she set her red timer for five minutes. (Our host—not the teacher—explained that each child had his own color timer, and that Jack's behavior of speaking out on irrelevant matters was being extinguished by this.)

A few minutes later a girl slumped down in her chair. Again the teacher stood up, this time to tape the girl's upper arms to the back of the chair. This time she set the green timer for five minutes before she sat down and calmly resumed the lesson.

Soon a bell rang announcing the end of the five minutes on the red timer. Up went the teacher, off came the tape, down went the teacher, on went the lesson.

And so it went the rest of the day during various lessons and activities. All was very painful for us to watch at the time or to recall and discuss later.

Why had our opinion of this teacher and her methods sunk so low? The answer lies in our conviction that a professionally-trained teacher, supposedly knowledgeable in concepts of learning and child development, should have known what she was in fact doing.

The following is an account of some of the negative learnings taking place there, where supposedly an outstanding program of behavior modification was being implemented. We also include notes on how this teacher was unintentionally (we assume) promoting these concepts.

What was probably being learned by the children:	*Unintentional teaching tool:*
1. To be good I must pay attention to what adults say.	1. Only the teacher decides what is to be said and by whom.

2. I cannot control myself.

3. When I get bigger I will control children or people who are powerless, as I am now.

4. My ideas and my work have no value.

5. I must stop looking at or thinking about things that really interest me.

6. I will please the teacher if I don't make friends with anyone at school.

7. I am so stupid that I cannot take care of even the simplest materials.

8. Life is a chain of frightening experiences.

2. The teacher controls behaviors.

3. Teacher exerts power openly.

4. No display of childrens' work or opportunity for child-selection of activities.

5. Covering mirrors and windows may have removed some distractions, but were not replaced with materials of real interest to children. What remained was a vacuum.

6. All task assignments were to be done in isolation, inhibiting normal social development and verbal interaction.

7. All supplies were handled by the teacher.

8. To escape punishment children conformed in a robot-like manner.

The list could be longer, but these learnings show how harmful this situation was to this group of children. If only one of the learnings listed above is occurring, there are some frightening long-term implications. What kind of husbands, wives or parents will these children become? How are they handling their frustrations? Will they become self-reliant decision-makers? Hopefully the program was terminated soon after we saw it; we have no current information. Hopefully also the children went on to more rationally conceived environments, where nonverbal and verbal messages were more positive and more realistically attuned to the "real" world.

This program was widely publicized as behavior modification, but the most fundamental of behavior modification advocates would disclaim it. We have included it to show two lessons:

1. Programs or materials can be labelled "behavior modification" without having anything constructive to do with the behavioral sciences. Don't be duped!

2. Beware of covert nonverbal messages being sent in your classroom, by the room itself and teacher behaviors.

WHAT SEATING ARRANGEMENTS SAY

Nonverbal messages are constantly sent from you to your class by the way you arrange your classroom furniture. Here are four classrooms, with the messages children may be receiving from each of them:·

Room A

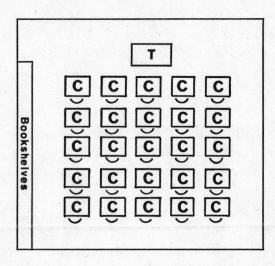

The child may receive these messages:

1. My desk faces the teacher; the teacher is the most important person here.
2. Children should not talk to each other.
3. I have my own place to work. I am responsible for it and for myself.
4. I will be working by myself most or all of the time.
5. The teacher will do most of the talking.

Room B

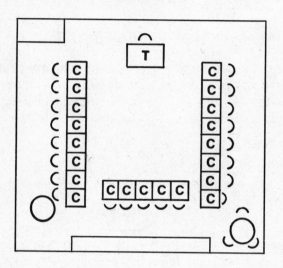

The child may receive these messages:

1. The teacher is a leader.
2. I will be allowed to talk and work with the children near me.
3. There will be some opportunity for me to work in a small group at the table, away from the rest of the class.
4. I will be allowed to move around the room to get materials or return them.
5. Most of the time I will work at my own desk.

Room C

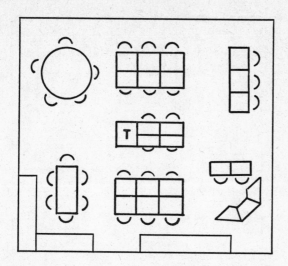

The child may receive these messages:

1. The teacher wants to be available to help.
2. Some children need to sit near the teacher.
3. Talking to children in my group is allowed.
4. I will do part of my work at my desk, part at the interest centers.
5. I might be able to change the location of my desk.
6. There will be a lot of talking and a lot of moving around in this room.

Room D

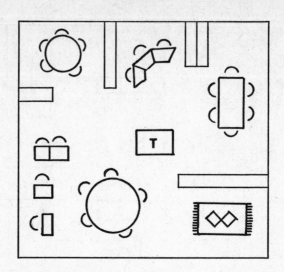

The child may receive these messages:

1. The teacher has her own desk.
2. I can sit wherever I want.
   or
   I may have an assigned seat but I probably won't have a "regular" desk.
3. I will be doing many different types of things in this room.
   or
   I wonder if I am supposed to know what to do here; if I don't know maybe I'll feel lost.
4. This is a good room for a grown-up kid like me.
   or
   I hope I can figure out what is expected of me here.
   or
   I can do what I want to do here.
5. Oh boy! With all these different activities I'll bet I can fool around all day and the teacher won't notice me.

6. This room is different from last year's—I am excited about what we will do here.
or
This room is different—I am afraid of new experiences. What will happen to me?
7. This room is not like the other classrooms. What will my parents think of it?

As you can see, the most traditional classroom (Room A) sends very clear messages about what to expect there. The most open (Room D), on the other hand, sends messages that are more ambivalent. Traditional settings need little explanation; more open situations require much firm and consistent teacher explanation concerning what is to be expected and allowed.

Note that both A and D have their disadvantages. In Room A, emotionally insecure children will enjoy the structure and clear guidelines, while more secure children will desire more freedom and choice. In Room D, however, secure children will enjoy the freedom but insecure children will need guidance to avoid receiving messages that are inaccurate or threatening.

For this reason many classroom teachers prefer an arrangement somewhere between A and D, so that the individual differences within a group may be accommodated. Or perhaps a teacher planning to run her classroom like Room D suggests would begin the year with Room B or C, or more like what the children would have had the previous year. Then, when the class seems prepared to handle choices and responsibilities implied in Room D, the furniture can be rearranged.

No matter how you arrange the furniture, your verbal and nonverbal messages must be in line. Nonverbal messages your arrangement sends must not be contradicted by your behavior or instructional program. Suppose, for example, a teacher arranges an exciting bulletin board which nonverbally says, "The teacher wants children to enjoy and talk about this display." Out loud the teacher says, "All right, class, get away from there and sit down." By not allowing a time to enjoy the bulletin board she is sending contradictory messages which will only confuse the children. They are being stimulated and attracted by nonverbal cues, but pulled away by verbal cues.

In this sense the classroom is no different from the world outside. The young woman who wears a seductive dress should not be surprised when men are drawn to her. The man who appears at a job interview for an executive position and is dressed for a hippie protest rally should not be surprised when he is rejected. And the mother of a three-year-old who puts the birthday cake and presents in full view should not be surprised when the child wants to eat the cake and open the gifts.

We usually think of instructions and guidelines as verbal. But in fact most of the instructions and guidelines in the majority of educational situations are communicated *non*-verbally. Therefore it is essential in any program of behavior modification that children receive consistent messages for the behaviors you are trying to encourage. Children need to understand continually what it is you expect and what you value.

DETERMINING YOUR TEACHING STYLE

There is no one room arrangement or teaching style that is universally best. Today's teacher is exposed to many different educational approaches, from permissive open classrooms to those which are highly structured and achievement oriented. All are supported by strong proponents. So far no single approach has been proven conclusively as *the* most effective.

As a result you are free to choose the framework that meets your needs as well as those of the children you teach. If you value (or require) an absolutely quiet room and teach a group that needs both structure and direction, you would be wise to set up an environment like Room A. If you can function with some group work and a bit more socializing, then you should try Room B. If you can relax while children function in committees and assume more responsibility for classroom decisions, try Room C. And if you can remain emotionally secure and satisfied while the class erupts in continual enthusiasm—with yourself more of a resource person to be consulted when needed—then Room D is for you.

SUMMARY

The environment you create for children will to a great extent determine their behavior while in your classroom. Begin with an arrangement you are sure will meet your own needs as well as theirs. Suppose you start in September with an atmosphere like Room A. Perhaps in a month or two you might want to group the childrens' desks for some activity periods or set up a reading corner. After a period of time you might find your room looking more like Room B or even C. The important thing at all stages of change is to keep the verbal and nonverbal messages congruent, so that you feel comfortable while communicating expected values and behavior patterns.

6 ASSIGNING TASKS TO PRODUCE BEHAVIORAL CHANGE

Most one room schoolhouses are gone. They have been combined into larger consolidated schools, on the assumption that third grade boys and girls throughout the town or district have much in common with one another. If the teacher were assigned thirty of these third-graders (instead of one or two) it was presumed she could use third grade textbooks to teach third grade concepts and make more effective use of her time.

But as schools were combined according to this pattern, teachers found that the system did not take into account the differing rates of development and modes of learning within that group of third graders. The on-grade-level materials were usable for about half of an "average" group; but perceptive teachers soon saw that many students above or below the average range were either bored or frustrated. To correct this weakness, many schools advanced or "double-promoted" brighter students and "retained" slower ones to repeat the grade. The purpose of this was to place all children in a setting where materials and an instructional program would be available on their level of learning. Here again there were problems, this time in the social realm: children found themselves in classrooms where everyone was from one to three years younger or older than themselves. Many, especially the bright ones, made the adjustment, at least outwardly. But for many slow students it was tragic; they often marked time until they were legally able to drop out of school altogether.

Movements such as ability grouping, modular scheduling and continuous progress open classrooms were all attempts to design an organizational structure with none of these disadvantages. Yet each in turn has shown some serious weaknesses. In some "progressive" school districts, so many different organizational patterns have been instituted, revised and discarded that teachers (most trained in traditional methods) are depressed at the very mention of *another* district plan under consideration.

In the process of adapting and changing, however, some schools have discovered and adopted instructional strategies of "individualized education." Many of us have had the impression that individualizing meant instituting another organizational plan, tearing down walls and creating a permissive atmosphere. An increasing number have recognized individualization for what it is, a philosophy to be utilized under *any* organization framework. More and more teachers throughout the country are individualizing, sometimes without even knowing it. Individualized instruction is taking place in rows and on rugs. Teachers are finding out that when children receive appropriate assignments within their capability, they experience continual success and have no need to exhibit maladaptive behavior or drop out of school.

Individualizing task assignments for a class of thirty may mean giving the same assignment to all thirty, giving thirty different assignments or any combination in between. The distinguishing characteristic of individualized instruction is not the organizational structure, but the priority given to the needs of the individual child.

This chapter will equip you to assign appropriate tasks to your class, regardless of your pattern of organization. It will deal mainly with those techniques practical for group work, with additional help for special problems given in later chapters. But whether dealing with a child or a group, the foundation principle is the same: when a child is given tasks within his ability, he will usually spare no efforts to complete them satisfactorily. Learning will result, along with a decreasing amount of maladaptive behavior if any has been observed.

BEHAVIORAL BASELINES

In the framework of behavioral psychology an understanding of *baselines* is a necessity.

> A *baseline* is the number of times any given behavior is observed in one individual within any given time period.

Baselines were first used in behavioral research to apply the structure of scientific methodology to the study of animal behavior. By tallying the exact number of times a certain behavior occurred under certain set conditions, researchers could measure the effect of any given changes upon the behavior being measured.

In human behavioral research, baselines are used to diagnose the severity of behavioral disorders and to evaluate the effect of various possible solutions. If Jeff is given a tranquilizing medication to correct certain hyperkinetic behaviors and those hyperkinetic behaviors *increase* in frequency above his baseline, one would probably conclude that the medication was not helping the situation. If a second medication is substituted for the first and the behaviors *decrease* below his baseline, one would conclude that this second medication—or something else—is helping Jeff.

The use of baselines in this traditional sense is much more appropriate for clinical settings than for schoolrooms. The focus is constantly upon the negative part of Jeff's behavior, an unfortunate way for the teacher to start having positive thoughts about him! (Someone else could count the occurrences of undesirable behaviors, but this is a nuisance and still leaves much work for the teacher.)

Because the usefulness of traditional baselines is thus limited, it seems constructive to create some additional types of baselines specifically appropriate for the instructional setting.

ACADEMIC BASELINES

> An *academic baseline* is the level at which a learner functions with success in any given subject or subject area.

If your whole fourth grade group is functioning *with success* at third grade level in math computation, then their academic baseline in math computation (as a group) is probably third grade level. If you use third grade materials to assign them tasks in that subject area you will have learning and success; if, on the other hand, you were to use second or fourth grade level assignments you would be using materials that are too easy or too difficult for them, and you would soon see various maladaptive behaviors, such as incomplete homework, disinterest during class or poor test marks. (Note that this reveals nothing about their academic baselines in other subjects like reading comprehension or social studies concepts, except when math computational skills are involved.)

You can also work backwards from student behavior to spot trouble areas in your instructional program. Which subject or subject area seems to bring out the worst in your group? What level academic baseline have you been assuming there? Is the work too hard?...too easy? Although there are many possible explanations for "behavior problems," these occur many times because the baselines set by the teacher are too high, or, in a few cases, because they are too low. Try adjusting the baseline you are using as the basis for your instructional program, either for the whole group or for individuals within the group who are trying to tell you by their behavior that they are not able to learn at that level.

Each September many teachers express shock and disappointment when they find within their classroom (fifth grade, for example) many students who cannot seem to function at that (fifth grade) level. Instead of blaming other teachers or the children themselves, these teachers need to remember the origin of these academic baselines. Psychological and educational frames of reference such as *IQ* and *grade level* were designed by using as a measure of comparison the ability or achievement of the "average" child. Statistically this would mean that half of the children given a test (throughout the country) would be above average and half below, with very few scoring exactly average. Educationally, we have adjusted this concept to say that there is an average *range* of ability; on *IQ* tests, for example, we have accepted a range of scores from 90 to 110 as average, instead of only 100. By defining "average" this way, one-fourth of the total (national) group will fall above the average range and one-fourth below.

The same thing is true of grade levels. Sixth grade level is the level of work that an eleven-year-old of average ability can complete *with success*—his academic baseline. So it should come as no surprise to us that in an "average" group, half the students will probably be outside the average range, in one direction or the other. There may be even more than half of the group that is not average, since few groups will be composed of this statistical distribution of abilities.

NON-ACADEMIC BASELINES

The social and emotional development of a child provides limits to the amount of academic progress he can make. Bill's independent reading (academic) baseline may be sixth grade level, but if he is emotionally unable to sit and read a library book for more than two minutes at a time, this fact is obviously going to keep him from applying his ability to read sixth grade level books independently.

A *non-academic baseline* is the psychosocial level at which a learner can function with success.

Included in the non-academic baseline would be the child's ability to attend to tasks with or without direct supervision, alone or with a group. It also assumes that tasks assigned are on his academic baseline.

Miss O'Brien's second graders are all about first grade level in their non-academic baselines (highly unlikely but nice and neat for illustrative purposes!). She has learned that she must be careful in assigning instructional tasks. Although these children know much subject matter at the second grade level, she knows they have not developed the attitudes, attention span and emotional capability to complete academic tasks of second grade level difficulty.

INSTRUCTIONAL BASELINES

The result of combining academic and non-academic baselines is a group's or an individual's *instructional baseline.*

> An *instructional baseline* is the highest academic level at which a learner can be expected to function with success in a given subject area, considering his academic and non-academic baselines.

This is not as complicated as it may sound. You begin by assigning your class work on a difficulty level equal to the best work you have ever received from them. (It must be work you are sure they did without assistance from *anyone.*) Then observe how well—or how poorly—and how long they attend to the task. If they function well in that level work, then the non-academic baselines are adequate for academic abilities, and this will be their instructional baseline *in this subject area.* If, however, they have problems with work at this level, try to observe if it is the whole group having trouble or just a few children. Then test out some lower level work on those who seem to need some adjustment. If attention improves, you are on the right track; keep adjusting levels until your whole group is working satisfactorily.

Sometimes it is possible to adjust the level of work without simply assigning "easier" work. Consider the case of Tommy, a third grader with achievement scores that show him working at third grade level. What the test scores do not show is that

Tommy is highly motivated and achieves such scores in test situations in spite of a rather serious weakness in the figure-ground area of visual perception. (This means he has problems with crowded workbook pages and complex pictures.) If he has difficulty with a workbook assignment and his teacher follows the above described procedure, she would assign him another crowded page but on an easier level. Actually this would eventually solve his problem, without the teacher knowing that he has this weakness. But Tommy could also do that third grade level page if the teacher cut it into smaller sections or taught Tommy to do this himself. How do you know the adjustments that will work for a particular child? You don't, unless you are able to have additional individual testing done, either within the school or at an outside agency. Meanwhile, you experiment until you find a way of assigning tasks that produces learning along with appropriate behavior.

Note also that when you proceed from one assignment to another, the abilities needed for success change, sometimes very subtly. A child may do well at a certain level with particular science experiments but flounder when it comes to writing the report. Is this odd? Not at all. All it means is that he is able to function at that particular level in the laboratory portion, but he will need to produce a report on a lower level, such as drawing pictures of what happens as in a comic strip or recording a narrative report on tape.

SHAPING BEHAVIOR

Whenever an individual is functioning below his potential in a given area, it is the professional responsibility of the teacher to try in every way possible to raise his level of output. One way to achieve this is by *shaping*.

Shaping is the guiding of an individual up a series of pre-planned progress-steps by raising gradually the level at which reinforcement is given.

The following chart shows how shaping was used to help Chris, who was determined, by standardized test results, to be an academically average sixth grader, but who could not complete independent assignments. It distressed the teacher to find that tasks had to be third grade level length and difficulty for Chris to work and learn. So she made a reading kit by tearing a third grade reading workbook apart, slipping the pages into plastic page protectors and placing these "cards" in a brightly colored box with a teacher's edition for correcting. Then she followed the steps pictured on page 94.

Long-range Goal Behavior: *successfully completing an independent reading assignment of 6th grade level difficulty.*

As you can see, the length of the assignments to be done in order to earn praise is gradually raised, until the long-range goal behavior is finally reached or until a maximum has been attained. When Chris finished the third grade kit, for example, she went on to a fourth and then a fifth grade kit. (Note that the teacher made these non-consumable, so she could reuse them for other children later.) By the end of the year Chris was able to complete a few sixth grade assignments with others in her class. In this particular case it was found that Chris could not stay in the sixth grade materials, because she started to show some of her old behaviors of daydreaming and wandering around the room. So her teacher resigned herself to the fact that Chris' instructional baseline was closer to fifth grade level, and she assigned her work there.

George's problem was slightly different. He was under great emotional pressure while his parents built a new home for the family. George withdrew from reality and refused, among other things, to read library books unless they were fantasies. One day his teacher began a program of behavior modification by suggesting a much easier book than he was used to reading,

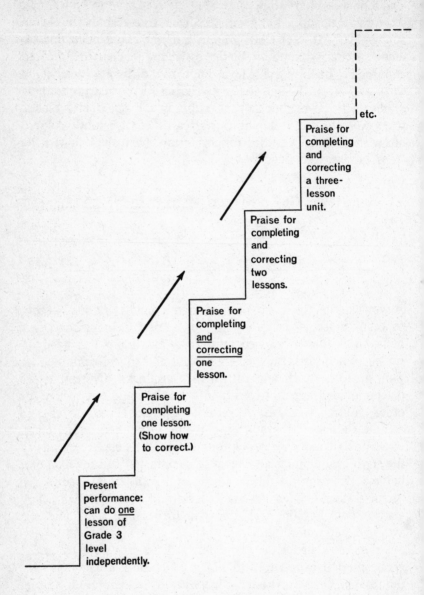

Figure 2: Possible Beginning Sub-Goals

but of the nonfiction variety; she praised him highly when he finished reading it. He continued to read easy nonfiction books along with some fantasies; the teacher praised him for the nonfiction books. When he chose and read a more difficult nonfiction book, she praised him again, this time raising the level at which she would thereafter reinforce him. Very gradually George learned to read increasingly difficult books about many different, exciting subjects, both real and imaginary.

THE LEARNING YEAR

Through this process of adjusting tasks to fit the child, we need some conception of the child's learning in terms of time, so that we may have some idea of how much progress to expect from him. This is most easily done by understanding a child's *learning year.*

A *learning year* is the amount of academic work any child can complete in a school year, assuming that the "average child" can do just about one year's work in a school year.

According to this a child with high ability would have a longer learning year, because he would learn faster and, if allowed to work continuously at his own speed, could complete more than a year's work in a year. A slower child's learning year would be shorter than the school year, since he would learn at a slower rate of speed and could not cover as much material.

If we follow along, only about half the members of an "average" class would have a learning year that "fits" the regular school year; for the others some adjustment in expectations and instructional programs—either upward or downward—will be necessary.

Here is an example of one child's school progress pictured in terms of her learning year. Jennifer is in kindergarten. She scored about 80 on an individually administered intelligence test, placing her well below the 90-110 average range. In a ten month school year, Jennifer will do considerably less than a year's work compared to her average classmates. As a result, Jennifer will need to use some of next year's time to finish this year's work. If she continues to function like this it is easy to picture how far behind her classmates she will be by fifth or sixth grade.

Jerry is also in kindergarten, but scored 120 on the same IQ test, well above average. His learning year will be more than a school year, and he will complete work in much less time than the rest of the class. What will he do with that extra time? Will he move ahead into first grade work? If so, what will happen when he finishes first grade work soon after the middle of first grade?

Although the concept of the learning year has some built-in shortcomings, it is useful in explaining an individual's potential to fellow teachers or parents. It is also helpful to remind us what a wide range of abilities are contained in almost any classroom, and how this range widens as children develop through the years of elementary school.

THE LEARNING RANGE

How then does a teacher know what materials to procure for this variety of individuals she may expect each year? What instructional baselines should be "normal"? The answer is found in the *learning range*.

The *learning range* is the total expanse of instructional baselines a teacher may expect on any assigned grade level.

Consider Mrs. Bragg, who teaches third grade. During the summer she may read this book and try to gather materials for the coming year. She should start by finding the average age of pupils in that grade; for most third grades it would be about eight years. Then she should find two-thirds of this, or about five in this case. The learning range of Mrs. Bragg's classes will probably be about five years, above, on and below her third grade level. She can expect each year to find children who range in achievement from that of a first grader to that of a fifth grader. According to this rule-of-thumb Mrs. Bragg had better have on hand materials and programs to challenge this learning range. (Some appropriate ideas for providing for such a distribution of abilities are detailed in Chapter 7: "Meeting Individual Needs in a Group Setting.")

INDIVIDUALIZING IN A TRADITIONAL CLASSROOM

There are many excellent books available on this subject, although most must be adapted using the framework explained in this chapter, so that practical programs with realistic expectations remain the central consideration. Among the few books that do not need such adaptation is, we believe, *Individualized Teaching in Elementary Schools,* by Stahl and Anzalone (Parker, 1970).

It seems helpful, in addition, to provide some practical encouragement to the traditionally trained teacher in the self-contained classroom of a traditional school. Since both of the authors have served education in that setting for several years, we have a profound sympathy for the problems you face.

Please proceed slowly. If you have now become convinced that you must change your present instructional program, you may gain too much enthusiasm to be realistic. Innovative ideas sound grand, but you have limitations of time, energy and perhaps administrative understanding. Start simply, with ideas and techniques you can see continuing for months to come. Perhaps a story from our own experience will illustrate what we mean.

Mr. Holbert was a third grade teacher who became frustrated with the lack of challenge for brighter students in his class, especially in math. The only materials he had were enough third grade books and workbooks to go around.

He chose from the class six students who were well above third grade level in math and also in work habits; he did not label this their instructional baseline but that is what it was. He called these students his "Math Stars" and put their names up on a poster on removable strips of posterboard. Then he had a heart-to-heart talk with the whole class, explaining that he felt it was time for some of them to work independently part of the time.

In this situation, use of letter grades was required, so Mr. Holbert went through the teacher's edition of the math workbook, making notes in the upper corner of each page to show what grade various scores would merit. (This had to vary from page to page because of the changing number of examples and problems presented. Test pages and those difficult for students to correct were marked with a note to see the teacher.)

All correct or -1 = A
-2 or -3 = B
-4 or -5 = C
More than 5 wrong = D

At the beginning of some classes, when a new concept was to be presented, the class would be taught as a whole. But on many other days the Stars would be told (in front of the rest of the class, so that others could learn the routine) that this was a review lesson, and that they were free to go ahead and do pages X and Y independently. When they had finished they were to get the teacher's edition and check their own work, noting the proper grade on each page. If any Star felt unsure of this particular concept he was free to join the rest of the class for that day.

This cautious approach was used because it was known that in previous grades these children had not received much training in working independently, so Mr. Holbert gave them as much responsibility as he felt they could handle successfully.

If a child received a grade below B on any page, he was expected to double-check himself: did he really understand the work? At any time he could ask to leave the Stars for a few days, and many did this from time to time. When children of high *academic* baseline but low *non-academic* development asked to join the Stars, it was gently explained to them that whenever they showed they could work well independently in a responsible manner, they had the academic ability to join the Stars. If a child received a grade below B for three straight days he would automatically leave the Stars for a closer instructional relationship to Mr. Holbert. Children were added to the Stars on the basis of grades earned (checked easily by flipping through the individual's workbook) and also their ability to carry through on independent work. Note that Stars membership was quite fluid, with no disgrace attached to leaving the group.

The above plan worked well as described. Grades in workbooks were used for an estimate of daily work the teacher felt was more accurate than the periodic tests alone. Other demonstrations of responsible behavior evolved, such as Stars offering to tutor students who had been absent or those who were experiencing some difficulty along the way. Because very little individualized instruction was carried out in that school, the Math Stars continued to receive what some would consider rather close guidance while their non-academic abilities were being brought up to their academic level. During this time, Stars began to use their newly acquired extra time wisely; many began stimulating study projects and extra reading during leftover math time.

Of course there is plenty of room for improvement in the above illustration—adding use of fourth grade math books and so on. Needs of low students may not have been met very efficiently. But the point is that Mr. Holbert communicated to the children that he credited some of them with superior ability, and they responded with increasingly mature work and behavior. For this unassisted teacher, this was a program he could live with!

SUMMARY

The goal in planning and carrying out an instructional program is to keep the motivation of the student high. Although it is helpful to consider the child's interests in this regard, even more important is making sure that all tasks assigned are within the learner's capabilities. The reverse is also true: when a child is faced with tasks beyond his reach, he tends to retreat into narrow areas of interest and other behavior patterns usually considered maladaptive.

7 MEETING INDIVIDUAL NEEDS IN A GROUP SETTING

Specialists concerned with childrens' educational needs may be divided into two main groups according to the focus of their pre-professional training. Classroom teachers are specialists who have been taught how to deal with *groups* of children; psychologists, counselors and their associates have been taught how to treat the *individual* child. Soon after entering educational professions those in each group begin to work with the other, only to find that anticipated help is somehow missing. The classroom teacher complains that he gives information on a child to the psychologist, but does not receive corrective techniques that are workable in his classroom. The psychologist complains, on the other hand, that after much time and detailed testing, his recommendations are not implemented. To a great extent both are right. It goes unnoticed or unspoken that training, orientation, vocabulary and job descriptions have built a giant chasm.

The bridge across such a chasm is the focus of this chapter. Classroom teachers will find ways to modify the behavior of certain children while meeting the needs of the rest of the group. They will also find here methods to develop independence in most children, freeing the teacher to observe and work with individuals. Although this book is primarily intended to help the classroom teacher, psychologists and other individual-oriented specialists should also find much guidance in the formulation of help actually usable by their classroom teachers.

102

STRUCTURE WHICH DEVELOPS AUTONOMY

The classroom teacher must necessarily meet the needs of the group before he attempts to help individuals within the group. He must establish a learning atmosphere in which the ground rules are clear to all, however they have been established. The most "open" and "permissive" of classrooms should have some routines which are agreed upon and enforced.

Within such a framework it is especially important to establish rules and organization by which the children will be allowed to use various classroom tools and materials. If you have ever tried to hang a picture and found the hammer missing, you know the frustration that a misplaced tool creates. Classroom tools, such as rulers, scissors, paintbrushes and teachers' editions must be available from the same storage locations all the time. Consumables, such as writing and construction paper, chalk, old magazines and extra crayons must be stored separately; this way it is easy to post signs about returning tools. It is also important to post a sign whenever a tool or material is not available at all, so that those considering its use will be advised to make other plans.

Once you have decided upon convenient storage areas, the next step is to decide for yourself the basic procedural structure necessary for children to work independently without annoying others in the group unnecessarily. You will not want a multitude of rules they will not remember, just some basic guidelines which you are sure will remain the same through the whole year. Even if you have not taught before, you can make these up before school starts in the fall. Here are a few examples of rules to prevent frustration and the maladaptive behavior that may result:

- The room will always be quiet enough for every person to work.
- In this room students always *ask* to borrow tools or materials from other students.
- Tools borrowed from the classroom supply will be returned to their proper storage area after use.

- A student who notices that a certain material is almost used up will tell the teacher or leave a note on his desk, so that more can be ordered.

As the year goes by more rules may be added to this list, but be sure each rule is essential for more than the immediate individual situation.

In addition to these basic rules, each teacher needs to recognize custom-made rules which he or she needs. These may accommodate his or her personality, or perhaps this particular group of children.

MODIFYING BEHAVIOR MOD

Miss Morgan, school psychologist, has observed and tested a child you recently referred. She recommends a program of behavior modification. From her highly specialized training she is already familiar with the literature on behavior-changing programs, and is sure the referred child would benefit from this approach. As she begins to outline some of the behavior modification techniques, you begin to project what using these will really be like. You accept the merits of the proposal, but you have very definite reservations about the risks involved.

You are not the first teacher to have such a reaction. Many suggested programs are never translated into action. This is due to a multitude of reasons, but a few relevant to our discussion are worth mentioning:

1. Most of the published and documented studies in behavior modification describe work done in clinical settings, not regular classrooms. Duplication of these procedures is rarely possible or appropriate anyplace but in another clinical setting. The classroom is not a controlled atmosphere in the same sense.

2. Tools and techniques considered basic to clinical programs of behavior modification would create unmanageable problems in a classroom situation. Common sense should tell a classroom teacher that

doling out candies or toys to selected children within a group will inevitably lead to feelings of jealousy and conflict. How would you explain any token system, for example, if tokens are given only to the children who create problems and monopolize the teacher's time?

3. In clinical programs of behavior modification, parents expect atypical techniques; they also delegate to the clinic or institution the *total responsibility* for the care and treatment of their child. Such programs would be difficult to explain sufficiently to parents if used in regular classrooms.

4. Classroom teachers are highly trained specialists, but not in the clinical approach. Agencies using behavior modification programs are staffed by individual-oriented specialists and child care workers, support systems not available in regular classroom settings.

Before all our classroom teacher-readers toss this book into the nearest wastebasket, let us hasten to list some effective ways by which classroom teachers *can* make use of behavior modification techniques developed in clinical settings:

1. Curriculum and special-study groups of teachers can spend some productive time and effort modifying clinical behavioral techniques for use in the regular classroom. Programs thus produced would take into account the staff available to each classroom teacher locally and the in-service possibilities for training staff in programs thus evolved.

2. Individual classroom teachers who can envision the application of behavioral theory can contribute to the literature available by presenting programs and reports locally, and by submitting articles on this to local and national periodicals.

3. A classroom teacher who can demonstrate the value of behavior modification by using techniques outlined in this book will soon find himself a resource person to his

colleagues. Time invested will be well spent, although many of the ideas are not all that time-consuming to implement.

4. Although clinicians appear foreign to classroom teachers, having them as speakers occasionally may help regular classroom staff to gain insight and motivation to use programs of this kind. While the *exact techniques* reported may not be appropriately outlined, there is no doubt that the *concepts* which have evolved as a result of research in atypical settings can be applied to help every child.

USING STRUCTURE TO CHANGE BEHAVIOR IN GROUPS

Since the classroom teacher must always begin by considering the needs of the group, he must decide upon a set of expected behaviors, about which the children will exercise *no choice*. This procedure is much more crucial to the classroom teacher than it is to the clinician, because in the regular classroom it affects more children, with less staff to cope with breakdowns in the system.

In establishing structure you must strike a balance between encouraging independence, on the one hand, and providing enough security on the other.

Mr. Ketter is an exciting and creative teacher. His children function beautifully in what appears to be an "open classroom" situation. Children seem to be—and, indeed, are— allowed to make many decisions about how they will spend their time. They appear to be working on a great variety of projects and are obviously very free to express themselves.

Mr. Ketter is somewhat unique, however, because of the rules and routines he decided to establish within his room. Acting upon his belief that there is a definite difference between freedom and license, he provided the type of structure he felt necessary. The following is an excerpt from Mr. Ketter's guidelines:

1. All finished work is to be put in your yellow folder on my desk.

2. All unfinished paper work is to be kept in your green folder in your desk.

3. If you are working and do not wish to be interrupted, put your Do Not Disturb sign on your desk.

4. If you want a conference with me, sign up on the chalkboard. List the time you signed up, your name, and the topic you need to discuss (or you may write "Private" for a personal matter).

5. If you are having a problem and cannot wait for a conference, raise your hand or come to where I am working.

6. All rough drafts are to be done on yellow paper. (Spelling and punctuation do not count. Get your ideas down.)

7. All work you mean to publish (intend for others to read) is to be done on white paper. Get help with spelling and punctuation; write or print neatly.

8. If three people are at an interest center, sign up to use it later.

9. Every personal possession is to be marked with your initials.

10. All marked tools will be returned to their owners when found.

11. Any unmarked tools will become the property of the class until ownership is established.

12. If you have misplaced a tool you need, you may borrow one from the class supply. Be sure to sign the Borrowers' List.

13. All pencils are to be sharpened before 9:30 AM or quietly at the wastebasket after that.

14. All desks will be inspected on Mondays at 2:30 PM. Be sure yours is clean and ready.

15. Large unfinished projects are to be stored on the shelves in the project center.

16. When four people are working in the library corner, you may borrow a book, but should return to your seat to read it.

17. If you want to serve as a resource person for reading, see me for a qualifying evaluation.

Each student was given a copy of Mr. Ketter's rules (more than twice this many!) on the first day of school and a copy was posted in the classroom. Needless to say, Mr. Ketter and his guidelines (called "Ketter's Commandments" by many) were the subject of many school-related conversations!

If Mr. Ketter's procedure sounds to you like the Army, you are close; he served in the Navy for five years. There he feels he experienced constructive discipline for the first time in his life. Having been a product of a relatively permissive school system himself, he was aware of the constant adjustments he had made in routines, from one teacher to another, from one class to another, and sometimes from one day to another. Along with the many pleasant and satisfying memories of that individualized and experiential approach to education, he remembered the frustration and confusion he sometimes felt, when valued projects were destroyed or needed tools were unavailable. He remembered planning independent projects, but also wanting more supportive guidance in completing them.

Mr. Ketter had balked at first with routines in the Navy. He came to realize that it was an advantage not to have to make every decision and began to value more highly those decisions he did make and to explore some personal interests he had never found time or energy for before.

The success with which Mr. Ketter uses his guidelines in an open setting should not surprise anyone who stops to analyze his rationale. His classroom reflects a modification of what he has learned about structure and order through experience. As a result he provides a consistent and stable atmosphere in which his children can learn and behave constructively, free to use their time for making relevant and vital decisions.

MATERIALS WHICH ARE SELF-DIRECTING AND SELF-CORRECTING

One way to provide structure and continuity in an instructional program is to use textbooks and workbooks routinely in every subject to develop basic skills. Traditionally these have been in wide use for many years. But, unfortunately, while these will work with some children, the pace is often too slow or too fast for others. Some children can read the text and do the suggested activities all by themselves with time to spare, while some others never do seem to understand concepts presented, even with much teacher support.

If helping group members to become responsibly autonomous is one of your classroom goals (and if it isn't it should be!), then their instructional programs must somehow be constructed to allow for functioning independently for sizable periods of time. This will mean some kind of self-directing materials or assignments.

The easiest way to begin if you have only texts and workbooks to use is to make up ditto'd job sheet forms for your most able students. Probably one-fourth of your class could follow this type of assignment:

Job Sheet for __*Tammy*__

Text: *Math for Today, Book 4*

Student Tutors: __*Norman and Hilda*__

Job __*# 1*__   Date __*Oct. 7*__

Number		Finished
1	Read and study page 4. Do examples 1-14 and 18-20. Use the Teacher's Manual to check your work. Rework any problems you have trouble with.	
2	Read and study page 5. Do #9-26 on page 6.	

Do #9-26 on page 7.
Check with manual.
Rework as necessary.
3   Read and study page 9.
Do #1-14 on page 10.
Do #1-24 on page 11.
Check and rework if necessary.
4   Evaluation Worksheet I. See me.
If you score 85% you may go on.
5   Read and study page 14.
Do #4-30 on page 14.
Do #1-24 on page 15.
Check and rework if necessary.
6   Use Resource Book: *Math for
Moderns*—Book 4.
Read and study page 42.
Do #3-12 on page 19.
Do #8, 9, 12-24 on page 20.
Use manual (on Resource Book
Shelf) to check.
Rework if necessary.
7   Use text: *Math for Today*—Book 4.
Do #1-40 on page 20.
Use manual to check.
If you got 34 or more correct, see
me for Evaluation Worksheet II.
If you got 33 or less correct, go
back to jobs 5 and 6 again. For help
see posted list of helpers available.
8   Evaluation Worksheet III. See me.

It is possible to design job sheets for an entire text in a relatively short time. Remember to vary the numbers of examples used, to avoid boredom. Using sample texts as resource books is an excellent way to extend your materials immediately. Because children are regularly evaluated by you there is little chance of their getting in over their heads.

It is important to allow all children to check their own work. You must begin by assuming that they will operate honestly, even if you have your doubts privately. Checking work must follow established, well-explained procedures, always the same. Just what you mean by "Check your work" or "Correct your work" should also be clear, since teachers differ widely on what they expect.

Job sheets should always be typed or printed clearly, so that tasks are clearly defined, even to children with some reading or visual-perceptual difficulty.

As children work through a series of job sheets, be sure you keep a record of progress. This will be valuable to you, as teacher and evaluator, and also to children in the class who need help from someone who has already done that particular job. An example of such a Teacher Record Sheet follows.

Teacher Record Sheet for Math

(Date shown is the date completed.)

Job	Charley	Jim	Valerie	Tammy	Lance	Patsy	Sal	Judy	Kim
1	9/20	9/20	9/22	9/22	9/22	9/21			
2	9/20	9/21	9/24	9/23	9/23	9/22			
3	9/22	9/21	9/24	9/23	9/24	9/23			
4	9/23	9/22	9/28	9/24	9/28	9/27	10/1	10/1	10/5
5	9/24	9/23	9/29	9/24	9/29	9/29	10/4	10/1	
6	9/28	9/23	9/29	9/27	10/1	10/1		10/4	
7	9/28	9/24	10/4	10/4		10/4			
8	9/29	9/27	10/4	9/29	10/5				

SKILLS APPLICATION PACKAGES

Some children need more practice in certain skills within the instructional program than is usually provided by texts and accompanying workbooks. For these children you need to provide some kind of additional materials, so that half-learned or mislearned concepts and procedures will not subsequently create confusion for the child.

Assembling sufficient practice materials need not be expensive or time-consuming. Begin with the samples already mentioned. Add a few copies of any discarded texts you can find. Add also a copy or two of your own text series of other grade levels, above and below your own. A number of publishers will sell or provide free correlation charts, so that you or student helpers can find pages on regrouping numbers or possessive pronouns in these other series.

Constructing learning kits of books or workbooks is a worthwhile investment of time for a district conference day or an in-service course, provided the materials are in good enough condition to warrant the expenditure of time. Be sure that any such materials are non-consumable; do this by tearing the pages apart and slipping each page into a plastic page cover. Pages may also be laminated or mounted on cardboard, but quantity use of plastic page covers is much more convenient and durable. The teacher's edition or answer key should be placed in the back of the box. Worksheets should be provided for younger children or for those with learning difficulties. The box could be covered with brightly patterned vinyl-coated wallcovering. On the front outside of the box tape or paste a piece of oaktag with very simple directions, such as these:

Math Kit

You will need:
  pencil
  paper (or answer sheet, in front of kit)
  Lesson Card #1

To do a lesson:
  1. Read the front of the lesson card.
  2. Read the examples on the back of the lesson card.
  3. Copy each example on your paper and do it. Be sure to number examples carefully.
  4. Check your work with the Manual, in the back of the kit. Mark each right answer with an "x" and each wrong one with a "✓".
  5. Put your score—the number RIGHT—at the top of the page. Draw a circle around it.
  6. Do you understand your mistakes? If not, get some help.
  7. Check off Lesson 1 on the Teacher's Record Sheet above the kit, beside your name.
  8. Place your paper in the blue folder on the teacher's desk.
  9. Return the lesson card and manual to the kit. Be sure to put it in the right place, so the next person can find it.

With younger children or less familiar materials, it is really helpful to ditto the answer sheet and the directions. Many times children get lost in the process or forget to space their work unless a bit of guidance is provided. With individual copies of the directions, children can take them to where they are working and check off each step the first few times they use the kit. If you do this, still post the first step or two right on the box, as a reminder to everyone.

You can make materials more practical by mounting the different units on different colors of construction paper or by using tabs at the top of cards. Anything like this will enable children to replace cards more easily but will take additional time to prepare.

Making such kits can be projects for volunteer groups. If you do this be sure there is someone who can print and spell correctly for any labelling! Make up a sample of what you want done, and make directions very specific.

INTEREST CENTERS

Science, art, math, creative writing: these are just a few of the subjects which may serve as the theme of an interest center. These can serve as permanent or temporary places for children to work independently at their own levels. They can be elaborate, with shelves and apparatus, or simply a table where you have assembled related materials.

One teacher covered a portable divider with how-to art project suggestions from the *Instructor Magazine,* along with samples done by members of the class. All needed materials were provided, boxed and labelled clearly. (For many teachers this might only mean keeping the leftovers from one year's whole-class activity for an interest center the following year.) Children could take the necessary materials and directions to their own desks. When they completed the project they replaced the instructions on the divider.

Another teacher began by collecting small cardboard boxes in the cupboard, each labelled with some topics she knew would be of interest: dogs, gravity, magnets, scrap sculpture. Then when she found a worksheet related to that subject, she would add it to the proper box. This continued until she had enough material in a box to constitute an interest center. Sometimes children would bring in books or paraphernalia to add to her resources.

A math center we observed was assembled by a team of children. It consisted of task cards and sets of materials stored in large manila envelopes. The following were some of the task cards and materials included:

Task Card	*Materials*
1. Estimate how many yellow squares it will take to cover the big red square. Do you know a quicker way?	15 10-inch square yellow squares 1 red posterboard, 30" x 40"
2. How many different rectangles can you make	Paper or posterboard cut into 1-inch squares

Task Card	*Materials*
using the squares? Trace the shapes you make on brown paper.	Brown paper, from paper bags
3. How many inches of string will you need to go around each one? Write the number in the middle of each rectangle in chalk. Can you find the answers without using a string?	String enough to go around the largest possible rectangle Ruler Rectangles of thin plywood Chalk Sponge to erase chalk

In addition to the task cards and envelope sets developed by children, commercial mathematics games, yardstick, counters and a battered adding machine were part of this interest center.

Some teachers allow children to work at interest centers only when they have completed certain tasks, while others allow children to use centers whenever they wish. We would suggest the use of interest centers as part of the basic instructional program, rather than considering it an extra. Children need choices, alternatives, if they are to learn to act independently and responsibly. For some children, interest centers can provide a safety-valve function. When frustration with ongoing tasks builds up they have an alternate way of using time constructively, until they are ready to resume work on the former tasks.

THE USE OF LOGS AND CONTRACTS

Miss Lokar teaches in an open classroom setting. All her children are grouped and regrouped during the year for instruction in basic skills. Most content-area studies (such as social studies and science) are done through independent projects and reports. There is an abundance of self-directing, self-correcting materials, programmed learning kits and interest centers in Miss Lokar's area, designed by herself, other professionals on the teaching team and the children. With so much going on each day Miss Lokar has found it hard to contact each child individually. So she has developed a daily log system.

Each child has a center-stitched theme book of his own. Every day the first order of business is for each student to write in this log what he plans to do today, along with how and when he plans to do it. She started with simple lists, then expanded logs to include an evaluation of each day's work. If the child is assigned to regularly scheduled skill-development groups, these are listed, along with any other instructional activities.

Each day Miss Lokar collects the logs as soon as they are completed. During the day, or sometimes that evening, Miss Lokar tries to add a comment for each child. It may be brief, but serves as the teacher's recognition of the child's effort. There is a firm rule in this class that no child may read another child's log, so that through the year children may become freer and more expert at planning for and expressing themselves in their logs. Because they *know* she will read and respond to their entries, and because their teacher is accepting of their feelings and attitudes, the logs have become a valuable two-way co-munication system.

If a child fills a log, he is given another, and the used one is stored. Over the course of days, weeks and months, patterns and degrees of growth are recorded. Occasionally the log serves as the focus of a teacher-student conference. If a child seems to lack the ability to plan the use of his time, additional help is given in this area.

There are relatively few incidents of aimless behavior in Miss Lokar's room. These children seem to enjoy and use productively both the logs and the time recorded there. In helping children structure their own time she is providing valuable experience in independence. The results are behavioral patterns of open communication and growth in decision-making.

MEETING VARIED NEEDS WITH OPEN-ENDED TASKS

One of the most effective ways of meeting the varied needs of children within a group is to have the entire group spend a part of every day working independently on *open-ended tasks*.

> An *open-ended task* is something that every child can perform correctly.

Begin a list, file or kit of open-ended tasks you can use to provide success for every child. The following list may help:

- Design a mysterious thing.
- Design the perfect chair.
- Tape-record the funniest thing that ever happened to you. Amy will help.
- Draw a map of a place where you would like to vacation.
- Design a boat you would like to own.
- My favorite TV program is ... because ...
- What would you buy if you had ten dollars?
- Design a car and write an ad to sell it.
- My favorite story is ... because ...
- Design a machine to do something you don't like to do.
- If you were a famous chef and were making up a new recipe, what would be in it?
- Design a Halloween costume.

These may be done or discussed as a group but are most useful when used as individual activities. In order to have open-ended tasks work for you, be sure to keep elements of competition from developing. Your goal should be to free children to express their own ideas. Once children learn that you appreciate and accept a wide range of ideas, they will invest more and more time and effort completing these assignments. Children often have ideas to add to your list; it is essential to have a long enough list in order that children continually have a wide range of choice, so that they are not doing the same thing time after time.

There are two important benefits of this kind of activity. First, it will provide you with more time for individual help, because children can do it independently. Second, you have unlimited opportunity for reinforcing positive behaviors positively, since each child's response will be correct.

CONTRASTING TEACHER COMMITMENT: YESTERDAY AND TODAY

Not too long ago the teacher might have referred the behaviorially-deviant child to a school psychologist or social worker, in an attempt to understand why he acted as he did in class. The resultant inquiry usually yielded an explanation for the behavior: e.g. the family has been having problems...the child was not encouraged to act responsibly at home and was encouraged to remain a baby to his parents. At the opposite end of the continuum: unrealistic demands were made upon the child to compete and succeed. A disadvantaged home was frequently overlooked as the experientially-deprived child was judged to be slow. Although all the reports seemed to differ, they shared a common and unwritten message: each child had a reason for behaving as he did.

Somehow teachers have had to live with that conclusion and try to tolerate what might be very upsetting or obnoxious behavior. Once explained and labelled, behavior became the teacher's problem, as though understanding the cause should automatically erase the problem and make life easier.

Times have changed, primarily as a result of the professionalization of teaching. Societal pressures for a well-trained and literate populace have also had their influence. Parents have been encouraged to support quality educational programs, and having provided the financial means, they feel they have a right to expect the proper results. Today's educator is no longer content with simplistic labels and explanations, nor would he be allowed to use them. He regards as his professional responsibility the task of developing behaviors which serve the individual learner best.

Ours is a pluralistic culture where children are genetically and experientially unique. Attempts to hold all children to a single standard of expectation have not worked. Today's teacher is asked and expected to provide for each child's instructional style, level and rate of learning, not in a tutorial setting, but with adult-student ratios as high as one to forty. This shift requires an entirely different classroom environment than has been the case in the past.

In a truly individualized program there may be ten or more instructional subgroups operating simultaneously within a classroom, most without direct teacher assistance. The frustration and attendant behavioral aimlessness which accompanies boredom and frustration will, in most cases, be minimized. It is essential, however, to develop programs which develop autonomy in the more behaviorally-mature learners in order to help children with limited capacity for self-control and/or a limited repertoire of behaviors for interacting with peers.

SUMMARY

Successful implementation of highly individualized behavior modification programs for some individuals requires a classroom climate where individualized instruction is the rule for all children. Utilization of techniques which allow children to function independently are essential if teachers are to individualize scholastic programs for all children. As a teacher your goal should be to have most children capable of working alone at their own levels and at their own rates, utilizing you as a resource, consultant and co-evaluator. You will be freed of the impossible and time-consuming task of trying to get all children working at the same level, and you should be able to devote more of your time to observing and interpreting the behavior of your children. Knowing more about the academic, non-academic and instructional baselines of each child will enable you to plan and carry out more effective educational programs.

For some individuals this may mean an adaptation of behavior modification strategies developed in clinical settings, adaptations which retain the concepts developed in atypical settings but not necessarily the same techniques.

8 HELPING
THE DISRUPTIVE CHILD

Jessy spreads chewing gum all over her face. She tells about trying to set her house on fire. She pokes others when going to lunch through the hallway. And everyone watches when she returns from the lavatory, because she is sure to make some amusing faces and gestures as she enters the room. Mr. Grant has never had a student like Jessy. Clearly she needs some specialized help. What can he do?

To help Mr. Grant and others like him faced with children like Jessy, it is pertinent to review what has been happening to disruptive children in the educational system. In the late 1930's schools began separating severely retarded or disturbed boys and girls into special classes in an effort to relieve the classroom teacher of this burden and to provide these children with what was thought to be a more appropriate education. Unfortunately this "exemption" from the regular classroom often amounted to a permanent sidelining of the child, many times in a custodial setting. Children who left the "mainstream" educational setting rarely rejoined it.

As parents of such children pressed for educational programs which involved more than baseball and basket-weaving, many dedicated educators explored ways to help atypical children. An increasing number of professionals came to view special class placement as the best if not the only way to reach and teach those with seemingly unusual needs. Many specially trained teachers joined the movement to set up various types of classes into which children with special needs could be placed.

Today, for a number of reasons, both teachers and parents are asking if this is the most effective way to educate these children. Is it right, for example, to virtually isolate and label them, so that sometimes as a direct result they are institutionalized for life? What if some of the testing is inaccurate or culturally biased? Isn't it risky to separate a child from his friends when we are not sure what his problem is? How much will he have to improve academically to prove he should be allowed to return to a regular classroom? Can we afford such programs when their results have been so unpredictable through the years? Many are wondering about the answers to such questions.

Needless to say, we think that techniques of behavior modification ought to be given a try in a child's regularly-assigned classroom first, so that special class placement can be limited to children whose problems have been identified or whose physical needs are clearly beyond the scope of regular classroom professionals. This chapter will focus upon the diagnosis of the most obvious group of children faced by classroom teachers, disruptive children like Jessy. We will show how to turn the energy of these destructive children into channels of learning and cooperation.

DEFINING DISRUPTIVE BEHAVIOR

Every teacher probably has boys and girls who would fit the teacher's own definition of "socially-disruptive." And no matter how many children were exempted from his room, the worst one left would be an annoyance. But every school has at least two or three boys or girls (most often boys, for some reason) whose behavior would fit *anyone's* definition! They interrupt group work, miss directions, distract their classmates whenever possible and punch people in the stomach when they are annoyed.

These children are the ones most often referred for psychological evaluation and help, since their behavior is the most obviously irritating. They continually interfere with the teacher's instructional program and frequently serve as the subject of lunchtime conversation in the faculty cafeteria. Year after year they level the most creative and ambitious instructional innovations ever devised and lay waste in an instant the plans their teachers struggled with for half a dozen evenings.

Because the antics of these children scuttle the learning atmosphere of a room, it is important to the teacher to reverse this type of behavior first. But it is just as important to analyze and correct other patterns of withdrawal and defeat, as described in the next two chapters. Disruptive behavior is the most annoying to most teachers, but not necessarily the most destructive to childrens' growth and development.

LIVING IN A DISRUPTIVE WORLD

The amount of emotional stimulation the modern child receives each day is unbelievable. When war or earthquake occurs anywhere in the world, he hears about it or sees it almost instantly. When floods and fires destroy homes and families, he views them in "living color," often while they are still flooding or burning. Such tragedies, which arouse the deepest possible fears in young children, have become daily happenings to him, part of his six-year-old or eight-year-old world.

Education itself has contributed to the upset within open classrooms or other organizational innovations, which sometimes remove from a child the possibility of predicting his own educational future. The result is a tense atmosphere, where insecurities are multiplied in both adults and children, and the least little word may spark a spontaneous burst of devastating behavior. Fortunately most children are able to react to these pressures and cope with them in ways that are considered socially acceptable. Some, on the other hand, come from backgrounds where aggression, violence and uncertainty are a way of life; these children turn to the same behaviors they have seen and learned as a reaction to frustration or confusion.

Since such a child has developed this pattern over a period of years, it will take consistent and persistent efforts to retrain him and meet one of the greatest challenges faced by the classroom teacher. A closer look at one such boy should lend emphasis to this point.

THE CASE OF DENNIS

Dennis is a fourth grade boy whose family could be classified sociologically as "upward-mobile-striving." They moved to their present suburban home from another state so that they could live in a lovely location where both Mother and Dad could work full-time and maintain this standard of living for Dennis and his three younger sisters. Although neither Mother nor Dad finished "grade school" they now talk about all four children finishing high school and going to college. Talk of college and professional careers distresses Dennis, who is having serious trouble making it through fourth grade!

Since both of Dennis' parents work long hours, he must get himself ready for school and also supervise his sisters both morning and afternoon. This responsibility raises anxiety in Dennis constantly, especially when one of the girls almost misses the bus. In addition, his mother is understandably tired each night and feels somewhat guilty about the things she does not have time or energy to do for her children. So she has become quite permissive in her discipline, allowing the children to watch a great deal of television unsupervised, which means they see innumerable crime-buster and horror shows. This adds even more highly emotional input to Dennis' life.

Since both his Dad and Mother were raised in homes where disputes were settled by yelling and physical force, they have tried to rise above this. So when they disagree they try to hide or ignore their resentments; they often go for several days without speaking to one another. Then once in a while, they let go and have a real battle, with Dad always threatening to leave if Mother doesn't admit she is wrong. Will he really leave this time, Dennis wonders?

Because Dennis scored Grade 4 reading level on a standardized test, this was the level of reading work his teacher assigned to him to begin with. What she did not realize was that although Dennis could score this high by checking multiple-choice items at this level, he was unable to do long reading assignments or write creative stories and research reports of the quality usually considered appropriate for the fourth grade. Dennis had no one at home with time, energy or ability to help him with assignments of this type. Since he couldn't do the homework by himself, he ended up not doing it at all.

When scolded by the teacher in front of his new potential friends, he shrugged his shoulders and pretended he didn't care. The teacher thought he *really* didn't care, and scolded more and louder. Poor Dennis was humiliated, but did not dare to let it show. When one of the boys teased him about the teacher's scolding he was embarrassed. Other boys joined in the teasing, and finally, on the way to lunch, he punched one of them. Now he became a good target, reacting visibly and violently, and often getting caught for the punching part of the episode. Since the homework assignments continued, so did the teasing and the punching and the getting caught. Thus one boy adopted self-defeating behaviors which would cause him problems for a long time to come, unless something was done to reverse the process.

WHAT THESE CHILDREN NEED

Although the particular types of disruptive behavior may differ from individual to individual, there are some basic characteristics and needs that apply to all disruptive individuals. When we see such a child in action, we usually regard him as a cool and cocky character. He appears strong and self-controlled, and thus a real threat to our authority. What we do not always see is the fear that completely controls such a person and his actions. Underneath that powerful exterior he is really a "frightened little kid." And the key word is "frightened"; he is afraid of everyone, himself most of all.

In analyzing and planning an instructional program for such a child, it is imperative to base it upon his needs:

1. He needs to feel that each situation is under control. This does not mean he needs to be dominated or closely supervised, only that he wants to feel there is someone nearby who is really responsible for the situation. (Conversely, he is apt to lose control altogether if he senses there is no one in charge; such a child is just *not able* to walk very far down a school hallway, for example, without an adult visible.)

2. He needs to feel there is someone to set *and maintain* some kind of limits for him. He fears very deeply his own power and destructiveness, and really wants someone to keep him from harming himself and others. (Some extremely disturbed disruptive children sincerely think they would destroy the whole world if left without control.)

3. He must learn to separate the *emotion* he feels from the *behavior* he uses to express the emotion. Someone must help him to identify the emotion he is feeling and show approval and acceptance of it, while rejecting as unacceptable the resulting maladaptive behavior:

   "It is perfectly understandable for you to be angry when she took your pen; you had a right to be angry. But hitting her was the wrong thing to do."

4. He needs to be instructed repeatedly and explicitly in how to deal with each type of everyday frustration. In the situation described above the teacher might then ask:

   "What could you have done that would have been better than hitting her?"

   The use of open-ended stories that parallel a situation could be even more useful, since it would include a discussion for the whole group and would provide help in an atmosphere less charged with emotion.

5. He has to have models to follow: teachers and respected classmates who know how to cope rationally with frustration. A teacher who yells a lot and loses his temper easily can really tear such a child apart emotionally.

6. He needs to feel continually that somehow he is maintaining control over his inner destructiveness. Thus he requires what might seem to be an abnormal amount of recognition for his successes.

WAYS TO ENCOURAGE ADAPTIVE BEHAVIOR

Disruptive children are so irritating that it is difficult to apply our basic behavior-changing principle consistently:

behavior that is reinforced will flourish. The automatic tendency in *all of us* when there is negative behavior is to admonish the person causing the disturbance. *Somehow, especially with disruptive children, this has to stop!*

"Significant others" in the class will still provide some reinforcement by giggling and laughing at such behavior, but even this will diminish if the teacher can manage to ignore the behavior she wishes to extinguish. With many children—especially younger ones—classmates can be enlisted to help. When the child having problems is out of the room, you can have a chat with the rest of the class or with just a few that seem to encourage him.

> "You all know that Peter is having a lot of trouble, especially coming back into the room quietly from the lavatory. I have noticed that he comes in much more quietly when I pretend I don't see or hear him. I know you all want to help Peter to become a helpful part of our class. How many of you think you can do as I do and just pretend you don't see the funny faces or hear the silly noises? Wonderful! I know he will be glad afterwards to know what you have done to help him. Let's try it all this week and see what happens."

In this particular illustration the teacher should be sure to check with the class somehow on Friday and commend them for helping so much. If some of his friends tell Peter what you have done, be truthful and straightforward.

> "That's right, Peter, and we all want to help you. I think you are much happier now that you don't have to worry about making all those funny faces. Don't you?"

A HELPFUL PROCEDURE

The following steps are suggested as a framework for a program to help a disruptive child:

1. Decide just what the offensive behavior is:
   - noise
   - interrupting others at work

- physical attacks on other children
- quiet but frequent physical movement to attract attention of classmates during class
- showoff behavior

2. Check the baselines used for planning his instructional program, to be sure they are commensurate with his abilities. If there is one subject or one time of day that is especially difficult for him, check this area first. Adjust his instructional baseline(s) accordingly for problem areas.

3. Resolve once and for all to stop reinforcing the offensive behavior. (Remember, you're reinforcing the deviant behavior if you call the group's attention to it.)

4. If the child destroys property or hurts people (including himself), say quietly,
   "I will not let you hit Tammy like that."
   or
   "I will not allow you to damage the table like that."
   Show that you control the situation. Often it will probably be necessary to follow this by placing him in the "Time Out" area described later in this chapter.

5. Decide what behavior you will reward positively to start building new patterns. Quiet work at his table for one minute (on a timer) may deserve praise for some children, to begin with; soon the time can be extended *very gradually*.

6. Establish some kind of chart or record, whereby the child himself can keep track of his progress.

7. Regularly praise him for any progress, sometimes in front of other children.

8. Continue the program long after you think it is necessary to do so, or the same old problems are sure to return!

WHEN SHOULD YOU PUNISH?

When this type of approach is suggested to teachers, the above question is often raised. And, indeed, why *not* punish the child for his wrongdoing, instead of maneuvering and arranging everything and everyone else around him? This is an important question to discuss.

The purpose of punishment has traditionally been two-fold: to point out to the offender that a given behavior is unacceptable or wrong, and to inhibit him from repeating the behavior. A third more sutble purpose of punishment—it seems to us—is to communicate to such an individual that the situation is not under his control, often a fact that he would subconsciously like to have someone tell him.

But if a teacher (or a succession of teachers) has punished a child over and over again for the same offense and the maladaptive behavior persists, then somehow we must admit that the punishment has not been doing its job. Furthermore something else may happen: the punished child may stop hitting other children but may start another behavior which he hopes is not as easily noticed by the teacher. (This is sometimes called *symptom substitution*.) In this case it is difficult to see what the punishing is accomplishing, except to vent the teacher's frustrations temporarily and reinforce the offensive behavior by calling attention to it.

Another point raised in favor of punishment is that when Arbie pokes his neighbors and we fail to punish him, but instead arrange his environment to encourage him to stop, we are pampering him and acting as if everyone else but Arbie is at fault. Arbie's classmates are the ones who are told to make the effort to ignore his pokes. While it is true that a certain amount of responsibility falls upon others in the group, the fact is that we have no other choice if we really want to get rid of his poking once and for all. In a truly traditional setting where discipline (meaning punishment, a misuse of the word "discipline" which is positive teaching) is highly prized, the reason so many children go through school with certain behavior patterns getting worse and worse is that these behaviors are recognized and reinforced continually, by both teachers and children. Those who defend the "good old days" sometimes forget that children thus disgraced were allowed to drop out of school at an earlier age, and thus it is only an illusion that "back then" children obeyed any better than they do today.

Having said all of that, we will agree that if a child destroys a book or a desk, he ought to pay for it. But instead of classifying this as punishment, we would much prefer to place it in a different category: in a more rational moment later the child realizes that he was wrong and wants to do something to make up for the damage. There is no harm in pointing out to a child the amount of damage he has done or in insisting that he pay for it: what matters (again) is allowing the child to control his own actions and be able to give himself the credit afterwards for having done something worthwhile. Forced apologies are harmful for the same reasons. Convince him to make the apology if you wish, but be careful you don't reinforce the offense by spending too much time on this. And be sure he understands you do not want him to apologize unless he is truly sorry.

TIME OUT

Many teachers reach the point with disruptive children when they dread another day in the same classroom. This is unfortunate, because it shows that the child is gaining control. But whether or not you enjoy having the child in your class, you must have a way of dealing with him at all times. When for any number of reasons you reach a point where you *cannot* allow him to continue in a certain behavior pattern or when you must act quickly to regain control of the group, have a prearranged *Time Out* place to use.

> *Time Out* is a place which *temporarily* isolates the offending child from the teacher and the rest of the group; it serves as an emotion cooling-off place for all.

Note that it is not a place of punishment, since that would be viewed by the child as attention and reinforcement. Time Out may be the school office, the health office, or—best of all—a secluded corner of the classroom itself. It must be supervised, but very indirectly and just enough that the child cannot continue the maladaptive behavior or injure anyone, including himself. (Note that a hallway outside the classroom would not meet this requirement and would in addition provide opportunities for the child to get into more trouble with children passing by.) He *must* not receive any lecture or other form of attention while there. He might be told something like this:

> "Arbie, I cannot let you hurt people. I want you to go to the Time Out corner with this timer and stay there until it rings. (Five minutes is a good length of time to use.) Anytime after that you may return to the group, provided you feel you can keep from hitting people."

Note that one specific behavior is mentioned, so that Arbie knows why he is being sent out. Also, you should keep in mind that one useful goal would be for Arbie to develop responsibility enough to ask to go to Time Out when he feels himself losing control. (This is why there should be no punishment there.) Soon he will develop an inward Time Out and lose the need to leave the group physically every time.

Remember: A child should never be allowed to damage property or hurt others. Time Out is an excellent way to cope with both of these occurrences, as well as many other times when the teacher cannot cope with the situation.

Is it wrong to use such a technique? Is it the same as admitting failure? Not really. As a teacher I am maintaining my role as leader, instead of losing my temper and reinforcing his old behavior again.

If several teachers in one wing of a school agree to use the Time Out approach you might find a mutually workable place to use. If so, label it plainly, so that other teachers will know why a child is there.

Having the child decide when to return after a minimum time is an attempt to have him begin controlling his own actions. If a child is unable to do this at first, you may have to tell him to return (if his bus is about to leave, for example). The next time you have to send him to Time Out give him the same instructions, hoping that this time he will return by himself. Chances are that if he does this consistently he is simply forgetting your instructions. In such a case whoever is supervising that area could repeat the instructions when the timer bell rings.

SUMMARY

If disruptive behavior is widespread in a particular class it may be that the teacher himself is constantly overstimulating the group: decorating for Christmas too soon, describing a proposed field trip in too great a detail, and so on. Somehow an environment is created where one or more children feel they must resort to disruptive behavior, because they know no other way to deal with their personal frustrations.

Adjusting the instructional program and teacher expectations is the place to start. Ignoring maladaptive behavior as much as possible will stop reinforcing it. At the same time reinforcing the type of behavior you would *like* him to repeat will result in extinction of the unwanted behavior and repetition of the adaptive behavior.

Use of a technique like Time Out will help a teacher cope with disruptive behavior without reinforcing it. This is especially important when a child damages property or people, since these are two behaviors not to be allowed—ever.

9 HELPING THE QUIET CHILD

Ron is explosive. Jane demands attention. Betty steals lunch money. But Tim causes no ripples of any kind. Quiet—sometimes withdrawn—his neat and correct work is usually done on time. As teachers we sometimes wish all our children were like Tim. The quiet and conforming child, however, may be developing behavioral response patterns which are as crippling and maladaptive as those of the socially-disruptive or defeated child.

IS THIS REALLY A PROBLEM?

There are some things that almost all normal children do: they experience frustration, they have a need to communicate with peers, and they develop definite preferences and opinions. Yet every teacher is familiar with the child who is a loner. Socially, he avoids interaction, preferring to do whatever is asked of him without exhibiting joy, anger or a sense of accomplishment.

Loners may come from any variety of home backgrounds, except for one thread of commonality they all seem to share: loners usually come from families where members or the whole family could be called loners, isolated somehow from the mainstream.

THE CASE OF JOHN

John is a quiet child. He is an only child, who stays with his grandmother while his widowed mother works. John is precocious in his ability to converse with adults. He has little enthusiasm for childlike stories, games and activities. John's mother is very proud of her son; he has not caused her any of the problems she has observed in other boys his age.

Recently some changes have taken place in John. He has begun to show some degree of contempt for his classmates. He appears sullen if the teacher fails to praise him for his superior behavior. He is also beginning to isolate himself from his teacher. At the beginning of the school year he constantly alerted her to the "bad things" some of his classmates were "getting away with," but lately he hasn't been bothering to tell her. She doesn't seem to care.

For John, school is a chaotic and required experience, to be ignored as much as possible. Home is his peaceful haven. Both his mother and his grandmother agree with these conclusions. "Times have changed," they tell him. "In our days a teacher would make everyone work and do something about discipline. Today she is probably afraid she'll lose her job if she punishes bad kids."

When John becomes angry at school, he clenches his fists and grits his teeth. While his achievement level is high and he conforms to all teacher expectations, John is developing a sense of fear and contempt toward many of the world's inhabitants. Furthermore he is building up a store of hostility and anger with time-bomb potential.

If, in later life, he is able to find an environment which matches his home in expectations and in seclusion from reality, John will be able to live his life with a measure of productivity. But unless something basic changes within his present home situation, there is a good possibility that some or all of the following behavior patterns will become a part of his daily living and life adjustment:

- John may continue to view himself as a "different male," better than the other boys. Lacking a strong male figure in his life, he may never identify with maleness at all. Many homosexual adjustments begin with early life experiences similar to John's.

- John may become increasingly set in his ways, compulsive about having things done just the right way. He is not gaining any ability to appreciate or evaluate alternate life styles, nor can he understand that there is any other way to solve problems or apportion time except his own. He is developing egocentrically in the true, psychological sense, since whenever he decides or does things at home, he is praised and reinforced by the two most "significant others." (At school, surrounded with persons he considers less significant, he withdraws, and does not even process available reinforcements.).

- John may develop coping behaviors which enable him to interact with peers in a limited way, allowing him to gain acceptance as a scholar or as a group member in work-centered activities. He may thus become the one everyone can depend upon, as long as the situation does not depend upon a capacity to carry on interpersonal relationships.

- Because John thrives on payoffs he receives when he conforms, he may not often try to express original ideas. If there is a creative spark in this child, it will gradually be extinguished, unless an effort is made to bring it to the surface and nurture it. John may end up ill-prepared for the rapid pace of societal change, which requires innovative and alterative adjustments by individual people.

- John may become subject to psychosomatic illnesses, because his repertoire of responses to frustration and anger is so limited. Since he continually chooses to deny he has these feelings, he bottles up reactions that would be altogether normal.

- If and when John's defenses break down, there is the possibility that he may erupt into violent and destructive behavior.

UNDERSTANDING THE QUIET CHILD

In general, quiet children face the same life situations as everyone else, situations which normally evoke human feelings and the expression of these feelings. By denying that these feelings exist, and by choosing to feel and respond only as they think others wish, they fail to grow adequately. The quiet child has learned by his own background of experiences and SR sequences to hold the expression of feelings in check.

Educators try to prepare children for life, through the development of skills which all humans need to function in society. Since the quiet child is usually achieving at academic levels in line with formal measurements of his capacity to learn, and is socially unobtrusive, his teachers often assume that he is proceeding properly along the continuum of educational progress. What is often overlooked is that his "good" behavior is usually a mere reflection of someone else's standards, expectations and values. In Freudian terminology he would be described as having a highly developed super-ego and a poorly developed ego. Behaviorally he does not exhibit a sense of self normally acquired by others through trial and error; he prefers to utilize the expectations and evaluations of others, so that he will be sure to meet with their approval. Thus he is also lacking in non-academic skills of self-direction and self-evaluation.

Easy to live with?—yes. Problem-free?—no. The quiet child has behavioral response patterns which are socially acceptable and seemingly constructive, yet often not recognized as inappropriate. Frequently the teacher is so involved in behavioral management of disruptive children and the provision of remedial help for children with academic difficulties that he does not have time or energy to look for problems where apparently none exist.

DESIGNING A BEHAVIOR MODIFICATION PROGRAM FOR JOHN

John was first identified as a child with problems by a counselor at a religious camp, rather than by the school staff. His mother had planned to attend a three week seminar to prepare

herself for an anticipated job promotion. Because the grandmother would be away visiting relatives during this period, she
decided to send him to camp. Three weeks in an orderly and
conservative environment would be good for him. He would also,
she felt, have an opportunity to form some friendships with boys
from good homes with standards similar to her own.

During the first week of camp, John unknowingly alerted
his counselor to his problems by his behavior. He rejected
swimming in the lake, because the algae and occasional debris of
this natural setting made him nauseous. Horseback riding was
fun at first, until he discovered that horses have habits of personal excretion quite different from those of his cat at home;
then this sport was equally disgusting. Because he insisted on
making his bed and straightening up his corner of the cabin
frequently, he began getting to meals late. He would linger in the
dining hall after meals to help clean up, rather than taking part
in the sports and other groups activities with his peers.

The minister in charge and the counselors held moral views
and values quite similar to those of John's mother, but years of
working with children made it easy for them to see that John's
"loner" patterns were somewhat bizarre compared with most
children who attended their camp.

At the end of John's stay at camp, the minister spoke with
John's mother, advising her to seek additional help for him. She
consulted her pediatrician, and then upon his recommendation,
a child psychiatrist. Although the psychiatrist found John's
patterns potentially psychotic, he diagnosed him as suffering
from an adjustment reaction of childhood. His treatment of
the situation consisted of working with both John and his
mother. With his mother, the psychiatrist would work on adjustment problems of widowhood and the single parent state.
With John he would carry out a program of behavior
modification cooperatively with school and home. Interpersonal
and intrapersonal behaviors would be the focus, with no concerns in academic areas.

Observations	Guidelines for Behavioral Change
1. John expresses anger by gritting his teeth and clenching his fists. He does not express anything verbally.	1. Provide behavioral models for John, so he can observe how someone else experiences feelings of frustration and anger and copes with these feelings constructively.
2. John uses value judgment words like "good" or "bad," but is unable to participate in discussions which tolerate any approval of value systems other than his. He is unable to clarify values.	2. Utilize techniques proposed by Glasser, *Schools Without Failure* or Raths and Simon, *Values and Teaching.* Schedule discussions with John's group on the judgments and values of characters in library book stories. (*Avoid using standard academic or world event topics.*)
3. John withdraws and remains silent in many situations when he is deserving of positive feedback but allows himself to be overlooked.	3. Do not praise John for quiet behavior. Be alert to more normal childlike bids for approval, and reinforce these.
4. John prefers to perform compulsive neatness behaviors, rather than interact with peers.	4. Pair him whenever possible with a non-aggressive and supportive child for tasks requiring neatness, but having some value to the classroom and peers, such as preparing ditto masters for record-keeping, carding and shelving library books. Co-plan with the pair how they will work together, and evaluate their work with them periodically.

5. John is unable to appreciate algae, mold, dirt and seeming disorder or discomfort.	5. Use non-text approach to science, pointing out the complexity and beauty of components of the natural world. Collect different colored molds, study the life cycle of the mosquito or analyze the composition of good garden soil. Encourage an enthusiasm for the real wonders of nature.
6. John is afraid of and genuinely repulsed by personal contact with some objects and most people.	6. Gradually desensitize him to these phobia-producing stimuli by presenting them first at a distance, then bringing them ever closer, while telling him positive things about the stimuli. (Remember, he is verbal and assimilates values from others.)

Since John was not exhibiting problems in his academic work *per se,* his academic program was to remain essentially the same. The focus of his behavioral program for the entire school year was based upon the six guidelines listed above. John's mother was to follow through at home with similar behavioral subgoals and reinforcements. (In order to allay her fears and establish a working partnership, John's mother was invited to observe his classroom; during these visits she admitted that her preconceived ideas of the classroom climate, based on John's overreactions, were erroneous.) Together mother and teacher evolved subgoals that would advance John toward a more rounded, tolerant and outgoing adjustment. They agreed to meet once every two weeks to discuss any progress and problems of their program as it proceeded.

THE DIRECTIVE PROGRAM TO EVOLVE A HEALTHY EMOTIONAL ADJUSTMENT FOR JOHN

The psychiatrist pointed out to John's mother that the one reason John seemed to be unable to express anger was because he never heard her or his grandmother discuss their frustrations or how they dealt with them. Thus this appeared to be an excellent starting place for her. John could be *told* about her frustrations and encourage to talk about his own. John had never been aware of their feelings, because their own adult attempts at coping consisted of denial or repression. They did this to provide a stable environment for John.

John's mother hated cleaning up the food and dishes after dinner when she was tired. Before this time she had been aware that while doing the dishes she was apt to be cross, so she usually told John to go and read quietly in the living room while she went about her work. Now she changed her procedure. "John," she said, "I really do hate to clean up after dinner. I'm so tired after working all day, and I get very lonely without Dad here. Tonight why don't you help me put the food away and rinse the dishes? I'll have someone to keep me company and the time will pass more quickly for me. I need a man around the house who'll help me out!"

This was not really a radical step, but it was enough to acknowledge her negative feelings and to include him in a plan to minimize her frustration in one area.

John's teacher decided to begin by working on his compulsive neatness. On a fall walk she discussed with the class the beauty of the individual leaves turning colors to create such a gorgeous scene. She also mentioned that she sometimes felt sad to think that summer was ending. As the children searched for leaves from various kinds of trees she noticed John's repulsion of wet or partially-decayed leaves. When the class got back to the room, she discussed with them the *wonder* of leaves decaying to replenish the soil. The class decided to construct a compost pile near the school and to keep careful records of the specific changes that occurred in the decomposition process. They planned to use the compost for their spring planting project: Mothers' Day flowers. John was first drawn to the idea of keeping the records and volunteered to make a chart. A collection of books on worms, soil and gardening were brought from the school library; science study projects were chosen from these topics.

Surprisingly enough, John ended up studying worms and their contribution to life and growth; the growth-death-decay cycle fascinated him. Interdependence in nature took on new meaning for him. John and a neighbor began their own compost heap; it was quite a concession for his mother to allow this in a corner of the yard! John participated in finding the beginnings of a worm family to inhabit it, although he talked his friend into handling them. When the friend's father invited the boys to go fishing, John's mother knew that she should encourage him to go. As John began to feel more at home in the world of fishing and compost piles, he and his mother worked out ways of changing clothes to keep the mess out of the house; she knew this was something she would not be able to tolerate.

Most of the procedures and activities described above seem like plain old common sense, things any family would just naturally follow. But for John's family the trauma of his father's death, his mother's heavy work load and his live-in grandmother created for them a somewhat artificial world where John was to be protected from unpleasant problems or feelings. Keeping neat, quiet and clean soon became a substitute for living an open and involved life.

In their bi-weekly conferences (which were later held over the phone) teacher and mother shared insights. John's teacher always alerted the mother to new topics she was trying to use with John. Once in awhile there was a quick call in one direction or the other, sharing some unexpected triumph or settling some question relative to their teamwork approach.

One such call was made by John's mother when she found eight plates of wet bread all over his room. They were labelled strangely (to her), "Garage," "Cat Box," "Basement," "Kitchen," "Bathroom," "Refrigerator," "Creek Water," and "Puddle Water." (She was proud of herself that she called the teacher before losing her temper!) The teacher explained that the class had become interested in molds and were using bread in the classroom as a medium for gathering spores at various locations. John was obviously duplicating the experiment at home. Both parent and teacher recognized this behavior as one which should be reinforced (praised). John's mother took him shopping for an inexpensive magnifying glass and they went to the library together for more books with good illustrations of molds. As the year progressed, John's behavior mirrored more and more his behavioral models. And the number of "significant others" expanded as his mother and teacher sought to encourage John's interaction with other students.

It was considered a significant indication of progress when John began to verbalize his frustrations and dislikes. He would say, "I don't want to do..." or "I get really angry when..." At this point the psychiatrist told them exactly how to accept the expression of feeling while helping him to learn how to cope with the feeling itself.

"I'm glad you've told me how you feel," his mother would say. "People often get angry when they have to...but that is one of the things children must learn. Perhaps you can do the job correctly but quickly, so you can work on something you like better." Sometimes he would set the stove timer for the amount of time he thought the "dirty work" should take, and then try to "beat the bell."

EVALUATING THIS PROGRAM

This case history is unlike many others described in that it required changing the behavior of three individuals: John, his mother and his teacher. It is also unique in that the original referral came not from the teacher or parent, but from an interested minister. It is representative of many such cases, in which someone interested in the proper development of a child initiates a chain of contacts and help.

Significant behavioral changes occurred in John's mother, who was encouraged to seek help for her son and to trust the other significant people in his life. This behavorial change occurred as a result of direct and didactic counselling and interpersonal communication: with the camp minister, the pediatrician, the psychiatrist and finally the teacher.

John's teacher learned to accept John's mother as a concerned but confused parent. John's mother learned to play her role as an interested and valued person. Together they could help him.

Note that in this case the program was managed largely by a team of mother and teacher. They set goals and contributed to the program from their own areas of contact and knowledge. Constant checking back and forth in person and by telephone enabled this team to work effectively, with occasional calls back to the child psychiatrist.

As in all of the other programs, the first people to change behaviorally were the significant adults in the child's life. They simply minimized or eliminated positive reinforcing of his withdrawing, compulsive neatness and conforming behaviors; at the same time they provided behavioral models and positive reinforcement for his expression of feelings, creative interest in the real world and cooperative planning.

SUMMARY

The quiet child is gradually retreating from a world he does not understand, relate to or appreciate. If allowed to continue this retreat pattern he will be left with an inner world of underdeveloped self and nothing more. Not having opportunity to reach out and process success or failure, he builds no reserve of experience, nor does he structure his own personal way of coping with difficulties. Instead he assimilates the values, judgments and behaviors of those adults who are "significant others" in his life. This precocious set of behaviors is frequently and unfortunately reinforced without a recognition of the problems it is actually revealing. Because they are not a direct result of the child's experience, evaluation and reevaluation, they are outside his process of learning and are non-functional, artifically learned behaviors. Behaviors learned in this way do not allow the child to adjust to the world and real experience. Programs designed to develop more appropriate behaviors for the quiet child must build on his ability to assimilate values and judgments of others. They must also be planned to include missing real life trial-and-error types of experiences to fill in the huge blank in his background. He needs behavior models together with verbal and non-verbal support if he is to begin developing rewarding social behaviors: openness, the ability to evolve his own values and the capacity to tolerate and hopefully appreciate the complexities of interpersonal and intercultural living.

10 HELPING THE DEFEATED CHILD

One of the most difficult types of children to understand and help is the defeated child because so often his behavior does not seem to follow an obvious pattern. He is a puzzling child, the one who seems to have "everything going for him," but who, for an everchanging list of reasons, never seems to succeed. He rarely exhibits either aggressive or withdrawn behavior, two of the most common patterns noticed by classroom teachers. And in any group intelligence or achievement test he usually scores a total of average or above-average categories. Yet in one or more areas he seems not to care about learning or achieving at all.

If this brief description brings a specific name to your mind, then this chapter contains material that will help you, for you are indeed dealing with a defeated child. Matthew is an example of this type of child.

THE CASE OF MATTHEW

Matthew was the oldest of four children born to school-teacher parents. He was an unplanned but wanted child who delighted his family with precocious verbal and cognitive behavior. He spoke in distinct words and then sentences at an early age and added comments to adult conversations which showed he knew what they were talking about. His motor development, both gross and fine, was slightly delayed, but seemed to his parents to be within the normal range of expectancy for his age.

When Matthew began kindergarten in a highly traditional class, he and his parents were surprised to find that he did not quite reach the teacher's expectations in his achievement.

Matthew could not hop on one foot, skip or draw circles in the correct direction, she said, although he was well ahead of the group in reading skills. His teacher spent extra time trying to help him improve motor coordination, but without any significant progress. Concerned, his parents consulted their pediatrician, who examined Matthew and found him well within all normal limits of motor development for a child who just turned five.

Somewhat relieved but still insecure, his parents decided to act upon the teacher's recommendation to help him at home. Life for Matthew changed abruptly. After years of being a source of amusement and pride to his family, he now began to view himself as somewhat defective. His peers, teacher and family reinforced this feeling by noting often how badly he needed help. His teacher tried to motivate him by repeating that a bright, verbal child like him should really be able to do all these things. If only he would *try harder....*

When a group I.Q. test was administered to the kindergarten class in May, the teacher was even more sure that Matthew's high ability should carry him along; he had scored in the ninety-eighth percentile, far beyond his classmates. Here she felt she had proof positive that he just wasn't trying; his daily work came nowhere near this superior ability. So she urged him more often to work harder in school and at home.

Matthew's parents became confused, torn between concern for their child and loyalty to their profession. Matthew would spend hours learning every word of Dickens' *Christmas Carol* from records he played over and over. He learned the names of great painters and much about their works and periods by watching a college course on the public television channel. In spite of this he could not write or even cut out paper shapes. Helping him at home in these skills became a battle: he was annoyed to have his other engrossing activities interrupted and became both irritated and tired soon after a help session began. At the end of his kindergarten year he could not—or would not—even color within the lines on a work-paper. His end-of-year report recommended that he repeat kindergarten, based on careless work habits and this lack of achievement.

Fortunately his parents decided that he should at least have a try at first grade, so insisted that he be promoted. His teacher thought Matthew a delightful child, destined to become a scientist. He learned to read easily and was soon placed in the top reading group. His writing was still messy with many words misspelled, but his teacher thought that perhaps he was just too impatient to take the necessary time to write down his wonderful ideas. Having him dictate his stories to her yielded "books" she placed in the classroom library.

When Matthew began second grade, all the problems of kindergarten returned. His teacher considered him inconsiderate, careless and a "smart aleck." Confused and weary by the end of the school year, his parents agreed to have him repeat second grade. After all, they reasoned, he was one of the youngest in the class, and maybe another year would help him catch up in his weak areas and become the all-around good student his I.Q. test scores indicated he "should be."

"Failing" a grade was the beginning of a "failure syndrome" for Matthew. He was intelligent enough to know what failing meant and to feel confused at the mixture of success and failure that now filled his life. This situation continued for the next three years.

Behaviorally, he was a child with unequally developed abilities. He excelled in oral language, concept development in content areas and the ability to perceive and interpret written symbols. Motorically he functioned years below his peers. Try as he would, Matthew could seemingly do nothing to gain approval in areas such as spelling and writing, activities requiring the integration of perceptual-motor skills.

When a teacher (knowingly or unknowingly) allowed Matthew to compensate for this weakness he could learn, work and gain approval. But when a teacher would focus on his weakness (dysgraphia) and institute an intensive remedial program, he could not function; therefore he could not meet the teacher's expectations. As the years went by he learned that it was easier in many ways to "not try and fail" than to "try and fail." Eventually he learned to say, through his behavior, "Look

here, I haven't failed, I didn't even try; I didn't *want* to attain
that objective anyway. If I had *wanted* to do it, I could have done
it, and probably better than anyone else."

Before we describe the successful program used to help
Matthew, let us gather from his case some thoughts to apply to
all such defeated children.

SOME GENERALIZATIONS TO HELP YOU UNDERSTAND DEFEATED CHILDREN

1. They have experienced a great many successes and
   failures, often both in the same arenas.

2. They have been expected *consistently* to perform tasks
   for which they lack cognitive, psycho-social, perceptual
   or motoric developmental ability.

3. They are confusing for adults and peers to deal with,
   because of their uneven development; they appear to be
   generally capable yet incapable, eager yet reluctant,
   bright yet non-achieving.

4. They are extremely sensitive to the expectations and
   evaluations of others.

5. Frequently they excel in a few rather narrow areas,
   usually those in which they have experienced success—or
   the lack of failure—consistently.

6. They become fearful of new experiences because of the
   sizable risk: great success or grand failure. They often
   learn to disguise this with a casual or superior attitude,
   pretending that they do not really care about ac-
   complishments in whatever area is being considered.

DESIGNING A BEHAVIOR MODIFICATION PROGRAM FOR MATTHEW

To keep our understanding of defeated children and their
needs realistic, let us look again at Matthew and examine the
program of behavior modification developed for him. It is
especially encouraging for us to do this, because of the delay in
starting to help him and the success which resulted.

During November of Matthew's fifth grade year, he was referred to the district psychologist for a comprehensive, psycho-educational diagnostic evaluation. The psychologist reviewed Matthew's school records:

- health records
- report cards
- teacher appraisals of problems and progress
- standardized test scores: readiness, group IQ, achievement
- reports of parent-teacher conferences
- sample papers

With these as background he met with Matthew's teacher, to piece together the subjective and objective records.

What they saw was a boy with the uneven development described in the last section. They also noticed the radical change in total achievement from one year to the next, evidently depending upon Matthew's relationship with each particular teacher. Furthermore, since Matthew had not yet sorted out his strengths and weaknesses sufficiently, he had a very fuzzy picture of his own total worth. When he found a teacher who accepted and encouraged him, he would work hard, often quite successfully. But too often he set his goals excessively high: evidently success in any form became too much for him to tolerate. When he inevitably met failure, he would abandon the goal altogether, reverting to a familiar and comfortable level and area of functioning. This would explain the lack of personal satisfaction that Matthew derived from his successes, and revealed a paradox: the teacher who had just seen Matthew succeed was ready to encourage him onward and upward, while all of a sudden Matthew was giving something a quick try and giving up, settling back. He devalued the areas of his own high competency, because he usually didn't have to try at all in these before he would surprise himself with success; yet in other areas he could not make even the *tiniest* gain, no matter how hard he tried. For Matthew the areas of competency and success became only a secure haven, where he could function with a known—if undervalued—outcome.

KINDS OF PROGRAMS

At this point let's step back and survey the alternative educational programs which might be used to help Matthew.

In planning educational experiences it is important to meet many different kinds of needs simultaneously. Thus, in establishing programs for individuals, it is crucial to choose the type of program appropriate for each individual in each subject area, and to evaluate continually whether you are changing levels and approaches as you switch from one subject area to another. Basically you can choose from three different types of programs in any subject area: developmental, remedial or compensatory.

A *developmental program* is a rationally-conceived set of experiences which advance the learner by levels, from zero through mastery. It is pragmatically designed and tested through time.

Developmental programs work for most children most of the time. Basal text series and curriculum outlines are examples of this approach.

A *remedial program* is one that identifies areas of specific weakness by testing the child as he progresses through the developmental program's continuum of subskills. It is tailored to fit the individual learner and to help him master each subskill in which he is found to perform poorly.

In general a remedial program focuses on the learner's weakness or weaknesses. High-interest-low-vocabulary reading programs and kits concentrating on skill weaknesses would be classified as remedial.

When remedial efforts have been tried without success you may assume that because of a perceptual-motoric disability, maturational lag or emotional problem, no amount of repeated exercise will accomplish positive learning. The child simply fails more often and more obviously.

A *compensatory program* is one that seeks other ways for a child to experience success in areas of weakness in his developmental program.

Compensatory programs are always built upon strengths. The use of Braille for blind or dyslexic children and color-coding musical notes for children with perceptual problems are examples.

USING BASELINES TO SELECT THE RIGHT PROGRAM

Because the psychologist was committed to a behavioristic approach, he did not administer any additional tests; instead he proceeded to evolve the following programs, based upon the baselines indicated. Baselines are expressed in terms of grade levels achieved.

Program for Matthew, Grade 5				
	Baselines			*Instructional Strategy*
	Aca-demic	Non-aca-demic	In-struc-tional	
Math	8	2	4	Compensatory program: use workbooks which require little writing and no copying to make up for Matthew's weakness in writing

	Baselines			Instructional Strategy
	Aca-demic	Non-aca-demic	In-struc-tional	
Oral Language	9	5	5	Developmental program: stress organization and reporting skills to use academic ability
Listening Language Skills	10	9	9	Developmental program: use multi-media materials from instructional materials center
Reading Ability	9	9	9	Developmental program: go on with a wide variety of reading at this level
Written Language	2	1	1	Compensatory program: use pictures and verbal reporting, develop dictation skills

In addition to the academic program outlined above, it is necessary next to list Matthew's psycho-social needs as expressed in his behavior, and to develop guidelines for a program of behavioral change that will operate in many or all parts of his instructional program.

Observations	Guidelines for Behavioral Change
1. For unexplained reasons this child is unable to perform many psycho-motor tasks.	1. He may never be able to perform these tasks. Accept this fact. Find other ways for him to show he has read something, for example, besides *writing* something.

Observations	*Guidelines for Behavioral Change*
2. This child is evidently unable to set realistic objectives for himself, or evaluate his achievements.	2. Design a program in which the teacher sets the objectives and gradually allows him to begin evaluation of his work.
3. This child undervalues himself, an inappropriate defense mechanism which should be extinguished.	3. Build realistic self-appraisal by recognizing areas of achievement and speaking frankly and openly of limits.

These three guidelines constituted Matthew's behavioral needs. With his background of failures and the large gap between decoding and encoding within the same subject area (reading), there was an urgent need to adopt an educational program that would immediately give Matthew success. For this reason these three guidelines were adopted as his *total* educational program for the remainder of his fifth grade year.

The next step was for the teacher and the psychologist to work together to set up a sequence of objectives to shape each guideline area. The shift in teacher expectations from traditional academic objectives to affective and compensatory was difficult for Matthew's teacher.

THE COMPENSATORY PROGRAM FOR MATTHEW'S INABILITY TO WRITE

First Matthew was told that for now he would not be expected to write much. Needless to say he was surprised and somewhat unbelieving. His teacher explained that someday perhaps he might master these skills, but for now it was more important for him to learn an equally effective means of recording and reporting.

Secondly the teacher prepared and gave to Matthew an outline for a modified research report. His first assignment was to find out as much as he could about the local public library. He was given books and filmstrips on techniques of slide-taking (available from Eastman Kodak, Rochester, New York). Taking the pictures and talking would perform for him the same function that writing did for others. Matthew used his outstanding verbal abilities to develop a tape-recorded narrative to accompany the slide presentation. Understandably his first attempts were acceptable but not outstanding, but he was bright enough to improve quickly in the ability to take the pictures and tape an interesting report.

THE COMPENSATORY PROGRAM TO SET OBJECTIVES AND EVALUATE ACHIEVEMENT

When Matthew first began work on his slide-tape presentations he was *given* clear and simple objectives, along with a timetable for attaining these. If he met the timetable deadlines he was rewarded on a chart which listed each step. As he completed each step he could check it, but if he did it before or by the exact due date he earned a *star* instead of a check. Furthermore ten stars would mean a special payoff. When he asked what the payoff would be, the answer was another question, "What do you hope it might be?" The teacher made note of his answers; she now had time to decide which suggestion would have intrinsic value to Matthew as a reinforcer and also educational value for her purposes. She decided upon Matthew's most enthusiastic idea, "A roll of film, to do what I want with." In addition she promised him he could then start work on a new slide-tape program on a topic of his choice. When he finally earned his ten stars she gave him the film and drew up a new timetable, this time letting him help plan the content outline and assume some responsibility for refining objectives set by the teacher.

At first Matthew used all the pictures he took. Eventually he was able to select only the best from each set he had taken. Soon he learned how to go back and retake pictures with which he was disappointed. And about the middle of the year he started asking questions like these:

"Does this picture tell enough?"
"Do I have enough pictures to tell this story?"

By this he was asking for positive criticism, a notable step of growth. The teacher would reply:

"What do *you* think?"
"Do you think it would be a good idea to...?"

Here the teacher was trying to function as a consultant: his would be the evaluation that counted.

By the end of the school year Matthew was actively and successfully producing high quality slide-tape shows. Some were good enough to become a permanent part of the school library-media center. During a family vacation in the spring he discovered commercially prepared slide sets sold at resort spots they visited. These he used with his own taped commentaries for shows on historical and geographical topics.

Throughout this program he assumed an ever increasing amount of responsibility for setting his own goals and establishing timetables. His teacher continued to elicit suggestions for payoffs, to be sure they had current intrinsic value. Teacher evaluation of his work continued to be limited to whether or not he attained his objectives along the timetable agreed upon. Value judgments were ignored until Matthew himself showed an interest in this phase of his work.

The feedback he received from his own classmates—and children in other classes who saw the shows—helped him to improve their quality. The fact that the other children continually expressed a desire to see his shows and do similar projects encouraged him and established him as talented in their eyes. After the middle of the year he helped other children produce their own slide-tape programs. His help in the technical aspects of lighting and composition were especially valued.

THE COMPENSATORY PROGRAM TO BUILD REALISTIC SELF-EXPECTATIONS

At first the teacher set all expectations and objectives for Matthew. Gradually—but not immediately—she encouraged him to assume just the degree of independence she was *sure* he could tolerate. At no point did she allow his plans to become complicated or grandiose.

The timetable for each project listed a date of expected completion for each step, and the date was checked or starred. In other words, there was no value judgment of the *quality* of work he was producing, only the timing of the completion of each phase. This was to keep the picture positive, so that he would not feel so great a need to defend and protect himself by underselling his own abilities. Note that reinforcements which began with checks and stars grew to include the respect of peers and the eventual acceptance of his projects by the school library-media center. Although the teacher suspected these would come, she did not mention this to Matthew; she wanted to avoid setting any goals that might not be reached and to let him have the joy of discovering some of these for himself.

CLARIFYING THE BEHAVIORAL ASPECTS OF THIS PROGRAM

A pragmatic appraisal of this child's program would show that this was indeed a high quality program of behavior modification, for the following reasons:

1. It identified and extinguished undesirable and self-defeating behaviors, replacing them with a set of predetermined productive and self-enhancing behaviors through the technique of shaping.

2. The program was totally individualized, with the baselines and strengths determined behaviorally.

3. Reinforcements which had intrinsic value (meaning) for the child were utilized.

4. The goals of the program depended upon the needs of this individual, rather than on attainment of basic curricular objectives which were irrelevant to Matthew and unattainable by him at that time.

5. Affective, psycho-motor and cognitive components of the boy's functional ability were incorporated into the baselines, objectives and reinforcements used.

6. This was a planned program. Although the goal was to develop productive and autonomous behavior in Matthew, the teacher maintained the responsibility for controlling environmental and interpersonal aspects, to ensure attainment of the objectives.

7. Desired behaviors were shaped over a period of time, with expectancies raised as often as Matthew could successfully meet them.

8. Activities structured into the program as it progressed were consistent with its long-range goals.

Insufficient time has elapsed to determine the long-range results of this program. Matthew is successfully participating in a regular classroom setting.

SUMMARY

Compensatory programs designed to maximize success experience and minimize failure are essential if the defeated child is to overcome the effects of a "failure syndrome."

You may not be able to accurately determine the cause of a child's inability to function as an *average* child would, but if repeated remediation has been unsuccessful it is likely that the child is trying to tell you something behaviorally:

"I don't learn this way."
   or
"I lack a specific capacity to do what you ask."
   or
"My bodily timetable of developmental growth does
   not allow me to perceive or perform this task—yet."

The *exact* message may not be clear and is not important; what *is* important is that you assume the responsibility for receiving a message of this kind and for changing "standard" curricular objectives. You must then develop objectives which...

   ...present attainable goals to that particular child.
   ...build upon his unique talents and capabilities.
   ...allow the child to participate in an educational
      program.

11 DEVELOPING A PROGRAM OF BEHAVIOR MODIFICATION BEYOND THE SELF-CONTAINED CLASSROOM

Thus far we have concentrated our attention on the self-contained classroom and programs of behavior modification workable in that type of organizational structure. There are many other organizational schemes in existence, such as open classrooms, team teaching, subject departmentalization and differentiated teaching staffs. In these non-self-contained settings, many professionals assume a part of the total responsibility for educating a child. Usually there is an attempt at staff specialization, but no one teacher retains the major responsibility for the child's educational program. The very opposite of the self-contained classroom is the open classroom, where roles of responsibility and authority are most diffused; obviously there are many different types of structure in between.

The underlying rationale of these settings is to offer each child a variety of adults and peer groups with whom to relate. This structural characteristic allows the individual learner to assume a different role and status within each of his instructional settings. A child who excels in analyzing literature may assume a leadership role in English literature class, yet be low man in physical education. Because the individual tends to do well in subjects which capitalize on his interests and abilities, he receives positive feedback while in that setting. In the ideal situation, the room, classmates and teacher all become possible sources of positive reinforcement.

PUTTING THE STUDENT FIRST

If programs of behavior modification are to work effectively in differentiated settings, it is important to remember that the concept of specialization was originally applied within schools to improve the quality of education available to *each student*. Although there are side benefits for teachers, such as fewer lesson plans to write and a smaller scope of curricular content to master, differentiation and departmentalization should not exist primarily to make the teacher's role an easier one. An administrative decision to modify or departmentalize is justified only when the intention is to improve the quality of experience available to each individual learner. Acceptance of this principle enables the educational team to select from a wide variety of educational settings those which will enable a child to grow. In other words, when a child has difficulty in a few classes but does well in others, the team should begin by determining the contingency reward system operating in *all settings* in which he is placed. Often the cause of frustration in one setting can be eliminated, freeing the learner to apply non-defensive and appropriate behavioral responses which he normally emits in low-threat environments. The selection of stimulus situations to serve the child are limited within self-contained settings; they are a resource that departmentalized settings should not fail to utilize. When a child is experiencing difficulty in one or more isolated settings, a team can ask itself, "In that trouble area, have we truly matched the child with appropriate resources now existing within our departmentalized organization?" Often a change in class assignment, teacher or area of concentration will eliminate problems of frustration manifested in inappropriate behavior. If very many problems of this type develop, it would be wise to focus on the problem area in detail, so that changes in organization and personnel can be considered.

USING THE OPEN CLASSROOM TO ADVANTAGE

Each open classroom is thoroughly equipped with a wide variety of materials: books, audio-visual hardware and software at a cost comparable to the expenditure for texts and workbooks alone in a self-contained classroom. Sharing of materials makes it possible to enrich the educational diet available to children, without requiring additional capital outlay. Teacher absence causes few problems, as there is always continuity of staff available to the group.

John Sargent, principal of an elementary school in upper New York State, describes his two large, open primary classes this way:

> "There's a vibrance in these classes. More positive things are happening to the children than was ever possible in self-contained rooms. The teachers are not isolated and the children are free to gravitate toward peer groups or to seek out a positive relationship with any of the five teachers or volunteers."

THE CASE OF ARTHUR

Although there are many advantages to the philosophy underlying open classroom organization, the following case will illustrate possible pitfalls in a program of behavior modification there:

The multi-age primary classroom to which Arthur Stang was assigned had recently been reorganized on an open basis. It consisted of 140 children, one head teacher, four helping teachers and two para-professionals. Music, art and physical education were taught in special rooms to groups scheduled on a twice-weekly basis. Pupil personnel resources available included school psychologist, speech pathologist, reading consultant and school social worker, each flexibly available a half-day per week.

Despite the adjustment problems of the staff to their new interdependence, everyone involved was enthusiastic. The staff had prepared the children well for the transition, and there were a good many laughs over happenings related to the period of adjustment.

One day Mrs. Johnsberg, the school caseworker, told the head teacher of this team that she had received a phone call from one of the mothers. Arthur, a quiet, achieving six-year-old was having difficulties at home: soiling his pants, wetting the bed at night and showing aggression toward his baby sister.

The classroom team's reaction was one of surprise; he had shown no signs of disturbance at school, they said. The team was confident that this problem was home-engendered and home-experienced, relatively unrelated to life at school. Arthur, far from being a problem, was an ideal student, the kind every teacher wants to duplicate again and again right down his class list.

Mrs. Johnsberg agreed to check back with Arthur's family and physician. Meanwhile Dr. Allen, the school psychologist, asked if he might observe Arthur in the classroom, just to double-check the conclusion that there was nothing to be alarmed about. The team teachers also decided to focus on Arthur as an individual and to take turns observing him, to be sure they were correct in their reactions.

The teachers found they were correct in describing Arthur as a "good student" in that he generally got assigned work done on time. But they all noticed some behaviors they had not had reason to see before. Arthur seemed to react to all single-task assignments constructively, but with a degree of tension and anxiety. One teacher compared him to a soldier on the firing line. He would hunch his shoulders slowly up and down, while swaying forward and back. Then he would draw his eyebrows together, purse and unpurse his lips and finally rub his head back against his shoulders. This behavioral sequence would accompany any anxiety situation. Then he would work for a few minutes, stop, repeat the stress behaviors and go on.

During story time and the discussion that followed, Arthur sat quietly. He didn't respond verbally to questions about the story; indeed, he appeared to be in a different world. Arthur was not a problem child, then or ever, in the sense that he "acted out" to annoy others, but as teachers saw repetition of his anxiety behavior, they suspected Arthur was a constricted, worried child, devoid of spontaneity. He behaved more like an elderly statesman involved in earth-shattering decisions than a six-year-old with a math paper.

Because of the complexity of the open situation, identifying the reinforcements which developed and maintained this behavior was difficult. Dr. Allen visited the class for an hour on three separate mornings, and he found capable teachers and aides working constructively with a large group of generally happy learners. As he observed informal and sub-group and individual activities he saw most children receiving praise and commendation from others, peers and adults. Obviously this classroom was doing good things for most of the children; positive reinforcement was available. He did notice that most children were operating independently in sub-groups without teacher help, and that most teacher time was well spent on children with learning problems.

Within all this hustle-bustle Arthur was an island, a spectator. He spoke to no one and no one spoke to him. Neither praise nor scolding came his way, as far as Dr. Allen could see.

As a result of his classroom observations, Dr. Allen felt it advisable to administer a battery of tests, including both intellectual and projective instruments. Results of these confirmed his opinion that intellectually Arthur functioned well above age-appropriate levels. Academically he was achieving at early first-grade level. Non-academically his personality development was more like that of a three-year-old. A picture of the social developments of an average three-year-old would really describe Arthur's psycho-social development quite well. Socially he was at the parallel-play stage; peer relationships had no meaning to him yet. This, added to his high intellectual abilities, produced a picture of uneven development which was as confusing to Arthur as it was to his teachers. He was not capable of setting goals for himself, or of evaluating his own performance. He still needed adults who would supply strong structure and guidance to fill this function. Only when a teacher told Arthur that he had succeeded would he feel success.

THE TEAM APPROACH

Dr. Allen and the other specialists presented their findings to the team involved in planning a behavior modification program for Arthur. The school social worker reported that Arthur's mother was a nervous, insecure person, who had suffered through school despite good grades. In the discussion that followed, opinion varied as to both goal and methods to be utilized; one teacher felt that pressure was coming from the home and there was little the school could do. Some members of the team saw Arthur's behavior as consistent with basic family personality characteristics, and hence irreparable.

Knowing that any program for Arthur had to be consistent, the group, including the building principal, decided upon a behavior modification program that would involve only three people: the one teacher to whom Arthur had already responded, the one volunteer who showed a special interest in him and Arthur himself. The total program had three key elements:

1. A clear hands-off policy was specified and agreed upon by Arthur's other teachers. When he approaches any adults other than those specified above, he will be referred to them *every time.*

2. At present Arthur is able to work for periods of five minutes in target areas, math and reading, before he exhibits the sequence of anxiety behaviors. The first goal is to increase this attention span to twenty minutes.

3. When the above goal is attained, then another goal will be devised to help Arthur attend to orally presented material.

Both the teacher and the volunteer working with Arthur were to confer with Dr. Allen once a week until these program goals were attained. In this way they could share observations and maintain a pattern of ongoing evaluation.

IMPLEMENTING THE PROGRAM

During the initial work-periods, materials in math and reading were modified to minimize anxiety for Arthur. Math worksheets were cut into smaller sections, each section containing one word-problem or a small group of examples. Arthur was presented with only one of these units at a time. Following each response (correct or incorrect) Arthur was rewarded with approving attention. If he became confused and added figures instead of subtracting, he was commended for having added correctly. Then the next unit would be presented. By carefully controlling the number of problems which Arthur had to contend with at a time and *reinforcing any correct aspect of his response*, the work-periods were easily expanded to twenty minutes within the first week of the program.

Arthur's teachers decided that the basal reading series he had been using was contributing to his problem; it was appropriate for his academic baseline but not for his non-academic or instructional baselines. For this reason they adopted the following techniques:

1. With help, he chose an easy library book, one which had one sentence or a short paragraph on each page.

2. The teacher or volunteer would discuss with him any pictures on the page and any word that was beyond his sight vocabulary.

3. Arthur would be asked to read that page silently and mention any word or idea that confused him. (He was not asked to read orally.)

4. Together they would turn to the next page; this time the teacher would read the whole page to Arthur, with little discussion. This was to keep Arthur's interest high.

Within a month reading sessions progressed beyond the objective of twenty minutes, and Arthur was able to ask for help without showing symptoms of anxiety. At the end of the month, when the educational team evaluated Arthur's progress, they felt that he now had an attention span appropriate for his age and academic baseline. In addition, he would now ask for help when he needed it, could listen to stories and would occasionally play with other children. From these observed behaviors the team concluded that Arthur was learning that school was a safe place and that teachers existed to help children.

The team then planned a whole new schedule of reinforcement for Arthur. In math, he was now given whole pages as units and was expected to work constructively for the whole twenty minutes. He would do a unit (page), check it and write the score at the top of the page (the number *right*). He would then be told how well he had worked and how carefully he had used the answer key to find his mistakes. Then he would get another unit and work on it in the same way, until the end of the twenty minute period. Gradually the number of pages he could complete during a work-period increased. Sessions were limited to twenty minutes and occasionally terminated when anxiety was observed.

The reading program grew along parallel lines. At first Arthur read only portions of books with his teacher. Frequently he asked to read more of the pages himself, until he was able to read an entire (easy) book on his own. Arthur was allowed to borrow any book he read completely; it was hinted he might want to show one to his mother. Mrs. Stang had been involved in the planning phase of the program for Arthur, but was pleased to become a more actively involved member of the team. As her son showed her each new book, she responded with sincere interest. She was encouraged to reread these books to Arthur but not to pressure *him* to read to *her*. When he *offered* to read a book to his mother, she was instructed to tell him any words that gave him trouble and to express her pleasure in hearing him read. Arthur showed a marked increase in "reading-to-others" behavior.

Arthur's individual reading time with his teacher was gradually shortened and eliminated; he was invited to join a group of four other children in a read-for-fun time. The goal of this activity was the enjoyment of books and reading in general; posture and enunciation were not stressed. The group met informally, on the rug in the library corner of the classroom. Children sprawled comfortably to read books they had chosen. Usually they would read silently (with an occasional chuckle), but once in a while a child would share a portion with a peer. If anyone had difficulty, he would ask a friend or approach the teacher. Arthur blossomed in this supportive group.

The educational team did not feel it was necessary to plan any further specific programs for Arthur. He did not join any of the formal instructional skill groups in math or reading for the rest of the year. In reading he was eventually placed in a programmed series, where he completed all the work in the first and second grade levels. In math he worked independently in a workbook, checking it himself with the teacher's manual.

He made unusual progress through the end of the school year, when his scores on standardized achievement tests were the highest in the class. By then he had read over 200 library books. Bedwetting and soiling had disappeared shortly after he started reading to his mother at home. (In all honesty we must admit that the aggression toward his sister was to disappear much more slowly; circumstances prevented the social worker from spending much time working with Arthur's parents on this problem.)

EXAMINING BEHAVIORAL ASPECTS OF ARTHUR'S PROGRAM

No tokens—candy bars, buzzers or shocks—are evident in this program; however, Arthur's behavior changed markedly. The planned changes and new learnings enabled him to utilize his intellectual ability in a satisfying way. A behaviorist familiar with desensitization would see in Arthur's programs the original anxiety-producing tasks (such as the math worksheets) exposed to him in extremely small doses, along with supportive teachers who served as non-threatening reinforcers. As Arthur associated small bits of work with a desired relationship, his tolerance level rose.

Note that even at the beginning Arthur had developed beyond the extremely concrete level. He was well able to utilize the support of his teacher as sufficient reward; he moved rapidly toward acceptance of intrinsic rewards, learning for its own sake. Arthur was also beyond the primitive nurturance level, making any token program unnecessary. Arthur's teachers were able to restructure the patterns of both stimuli and reinforcement for the benefit of Arthur's behavior and outlook by utilizing this child's strengths—*starting from where he was.*

SUMMARY

Such administrative organizational planning affords strengths and weaknesses to the teacher concerned with rational approaches to the development of individuals. Effective behavior modification programs succeed because they are individually conceived and administered.

The open classroom described incorporates many of the complexities found in non-self-contained settings. To provide programs of behavior modification for children in open settings, the following steps should be taken:

1. In gathering data, utilize all available professionals.

2. Limit the number of "significant other" adults to whom the child is expected to relate.

3. After establishing appropriate instructional baselines, use small units of instructional material.

4. Shape behavior cautiously, using many short-range goals to reach the long-range behavioral goals.

12 USING SCHOOL AND HOME RESOURCES TO BETTER ADVANTAGE

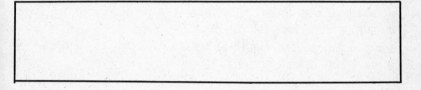

When you first try techniques of behavior modification, you will probably feel most comfortable using them by yourself, without having to depend on help or evaluation from your colleagues. But as you become more confident of your own capabilities in changing the behavior of your children, you will want to explore the wealth of professional help available to you beyond your own classroom.

MAKING USE OF YOUR FELLOW TEACHERS

The composite skills of any building's staff are bound to be richer than any one individual member's. Frequently staffs depend upon the building principal to bring about constructive interaction. The problem with this pattern is that the need for interpersonal growth goes far beyond what one administrator in a building can accomplish. If the climate of your building has not allowed for the free exchange of strengths and talents, begin informally to reach out to your fellow-teachers.

Many times a teacher assigned to a regular classroom has done extensive graduate work or has had prior experience in some specific field of interest. This background qualifies him as a resource person in a specific area of expertise. These professionals are frequently able to make valuable contributions in understanding children with unusual needs and in planning special programs for them.

It is only logical first to consider as resources the teachers who are working most closely at hand. Many schools use some form of tandem, team or departmentalized arrangement, especially for children in grades four through six and beyond. Since programs of behavior modification will be set up, carried on and evaluated differently from those in self-contained classrooms, it is important to recognize both the resources and the limitations accompanying such arrangements.

A self-contained classroom is a somewhat controlled atmosphere, at least when compared to any team or departmental setting. Results of behavior modification programs in such team situations are dependent upon the instigating teacher enlisting help from other professionals who deal with the child on a regular basis. In this way procedures will be standardized as much as possible.

For many children with learning problems the change from one classroom to another in non-self-contained settings is more of an adjustment than they can make, even if the "rules of operation" are approximately the same. A psychologist would say that these children have extreme difficulty with transitions. Sometimes arranging to have this type of child paired with a more mature and supportive peer will totally eliminate the problem; sometimes if the teacher accompanies a child part-way to his next class, that next teacher can meet him there or at least smile at him from his doorway. (Beware! This kind of arrangement often degenerates; be assured that if it does, the old behavior patterns will return!) These and other techniques can smooth the way for a child to be positively reinforced in his transitions.

When two teachers work as a team in a behavior modification program, it is essential that they continually work closely and consistently with one another. When they do this they more than double the results that one would obtain, since the child will be receiving consistent reinforcement for a larger percentage of the day. If a larger number of teachers is involved, it is that much more imperative that complete cooperation and consistency permeate the child's atmosphere.

Often a bit of communication will bring you all the cooperation you need. Marty had trouble with any fine-muscle activities and grew to dislike his art class, when this type of activity was basic to the success of the project. When Marty's teacher explained the situation to the art teacher, she was more than glad to have Marty work on an alternate project more satisfying to him.

Susan was artistic, but her teacher could not stand all the mess involved in creative art sessions beyond the regular classes with the art teacher. One of the other third grade teachers had a special interest in art and invited Susan to attend her weekly classroom art classes—she didn't mind the mess at all. This other teacher also provided Susan's teacher with a great deal of help, suggesting ways to use Susan's artistic talent in her own classroom: designing a cover for a social studies class booklet, planning a bulletin board and decorating the teacher's desk for the coming of spring.

All that Beth needed was a little walk once in a while to relax her and relieve the emotional tension she seemed to build up in her science class. The librarian was glad to have Beth come down to her for the second half of every science period to read a book or look at a film loop. Beth's teacher explained to her that she was not being punished. At first her teacher was afraid that Beth would take advantage of the situation; on the contrary, she worked harder than ever and sometimes even finished the full period's work in half the time!

In one school a chart was posted in the teachers' room on which such help could be requested in want-ad style.

Sometimes teachers' help can also be enlisted to switch a child's classroom assignment to overcome a clash of personalities between teacher and student or between two students.

Every school is different and so is every group of teachers. Think of the kind of help you need most and then start asking your fellow teachers for it.

USING THE EXPERTISE OF SPECIALISTS

There is a wide range in the amount and variety of highly specialized help available to classroom teachers. For example, some districts employ a reading resource teacher for every building, while others may not even provide a reading coordinator for the whole district. But in almost every district and for almost every classroom teacher there is *some* kind of staff help you can utilize.

Start by analyzing the specialized help you have at hand right in your own building. We have already mentioned your fellow-teachers, many of whom are talented and highly skilled in a variety of areas. Then take a good long look at the official list of district-shared personnel. Don't overlook anyone; the Audio-Visual Coordinator or the Elementary Supervisor may be looking for a way to promote more contact with classrooms directly. They or others may be able and willing to supply just the help you need.

In using the expertise of specialists, be careful to use them appropriately. First of all, use the correct specialist for the specific problem you are working on. If a child's behavior problems are really stemming from his noticeable speech defect, it is senseless and inefficient to consult the school psychologist before you have spoken with the speech therapist. We observed a teacher recently who fell into a habit of pleading for help from every specialist who came along; fortunately, in this case, the specialists happened to compare notes and were able to correct the situation. Secondly, you should watch the amount of time you expect to receive from these staff members. If a social case worker serves seven schools, you should not expect the equivalent of a half-day per week with you or your problems. Such professionals are usually more than willing to arrange their schedules according to your needs, but you should be reasonable, realistic and considerate in your demands upon their time. Thirdly, think how you can get the best possible use of their time. A psychologist might have to decide, for example, whether to test one child and write a full report, or to test three children and report orally to the teacher. In some districts the procedure (such as the written report) would be required of him, but in some places he can make the choice as to what type of help is needed most desperately. Often you can tell a psychologist the total number of children (right now) that you can see need some expert help. Then he can advise you as to the best use of his time. Or use him as a resource to your team of teachers at a faculty (team) meeting. This is especially useful if a specialist's time has been reduced to a very small amount per week in your building.

ESTABLISHING A MENTAL HEALTH TEAM

One very useful way of using specialists' talents effectively is to work toward some kind of team approach to behavioral problems in your school. One elementary school we have observed conducted a "clinic" every Tuesday afternoon, to which the following specialists went regularly:

- Building principal
- Counselor (shared by three schools)
- District psychologist (shared by three schools)
- District social worker (shared by seven schools)
- Nurse-Teacher (shared by three schools)
- Speech therapist (shared by three schools)
- Reading resource teacher (full-time in this building)
- Music teacher (full-time in this building, attending Mental Health team meetings voluntarily, out of a professional desire to learn more about individual children with problems and how to deal with them)

Although this "clinic" was not run on a basis we would call totally behavioral, it was quite effective in meeting with classroom teachers one by one to provide specialized help and advice.

A classroom teacher would sign up for a half-hour block of the team's time. He would note the names of one to three children with whom he needed help. Since the building schedule required all special area classes to end twenty minutes before dismissal, it was natural for the team to decide to meet during that time; they would discuss any cases pending or procedural questions. Then at dismissal time the first classroom teacher would join the group for his half-hour consultation.

Specialists would bring to the meeting any relevant records, and the group would ask the classroom teacher to explain the problem. Team members having some previous experience with the family or with that particular child would share any information or insights. By allowing the teacher to verbalize his problems and by analyzing these problems in the light of all available information, the team sought to find the probable source of the child's difficulty. It was often possible to do this and to suggest to the teacher some ways in which he might try dealing with the situation. In such cases an appointment might be made for a brief return conference with the team a month hence, to see if all was progressing as projected.

In many cases, however, more help than this was needed. Together, the team and the teacher would try to sort out the child's strengths and weaknesses in order to narrow down the areas for investigation. Perhaps the psychologist might be asked to observe the child in the classroom, and the speech therapist to screen his oral language, while the classroom teacher tried having him meet with two different reading groups. Or perhaps the social case worker might be asked to visit with the parents and seek to explore home conditions and the child's behavior while there. Whatever the course decided upon, the classroom teacher was given support while fellow-professionals helped determine what type of diagnosis or treatment procedures were appropriate.

By referring children with problems through one team like this, efficient use was made of special area resources. In the work of this particular team, reports and overlooked test results from former years were often uncovered, especially in areas where personnel had changed recently. And because each individual case was given such careful consideration, a leavening effect of support and partnership began to emerge between classroom teachers and specialists.

In terms of money, this was an expensive meeting for the district to support. But in terms of time, this group was really economical. Much overlapping and unnecessary testing was eliminated. If one specialist needed to contact another personally about a particular child, all of them knew they could do this any Tuesday afternoon. Written messages are appropriate much of the time for such communications, but often what is needed is personal consultation. This mental health team served the faculty of this building well in terms of actual practical help given.

Specialists serving more than two buildings may be reluctant to participate in such a program, feeling that some problems discussed may not concern them directly. But we have seen how such an agency can improve the working relationship of specialists with classroom teachers by regular participation in such a group. Furthermore if specialists knew that the classroom teachers of a building would support such an expenditure of time, they would be much more receptive to the idea than if they thought there would be opposition or a reluctance to use the team.

MAKING BEST USE OF ADULTS: AIDES, VOLUNTEERS AND OTHERS

There are often adults working in school situations who do not have the expertise to teach. But they have an interest in helping children, often a love for those they may hardly know. These adults can, in a variety of roles, often supply the stabilizing, consistent reinforcement that you need. Having someone with time to work with an individual student or with the opportunity to reach him in a different setting can be a real "plus" in your program. These folks can also sometimes perform some of the clerical tasks involved in teaching, relieving you to work more with individual children.

Whatever use you do make of these adults, be sure at all times that they are *contributing* to the carrying out of your programs of behavior modification. A volunteer who answers every question for a child who needs to be ignored temporarily is *no help!* On the other hand, having someone to get more worksheets or run off a ditto stencil can be a lifesaver.

We observed a reading lab where volunteers were used to great advantage. Some could only come in for an hour a week (one class plus clean-up time), but each was greatly appreciated. Volunteers worked under the very capable leadership of a chairman (volunteer), who came in to start each new volunteer.

They were instructed to sit at a designated table and remain there to correct certain crucial pre- and post-tests. Some volunteers could easily have expanded their responsibility, but it seemed best to the director of the reading lab to use the volunteers uniformly, so that they could switch classes or days without causing problems for teachers or students. As it was, such changes could be made and everyone in the situation knew what to expect each time.

Often parents are glad to help at school if they are sure their help is wanted. When they cannot help on a regular basis some kind of centralized volunteer bureau is needed, so that this does not take the teacher's time. Many books and pamphlets are available to give more detailed help in setting up such an organization.

Many teachers have said that they don't know what they would do without their aide(s). Of course we learn to depend on such help when it is available, once we learn to use it correctly. Sometimes such help could be made available if a group of classroom teachers could show (on paper) how her services would be used. If you are able to gain the services of such people, find out what their talents are and use them accordingly. Certain skills (such as typing) may be part of the basic job description; beyond that some have more ability to work with children than others.

A readily available category of help is the clerical, cafeteria and maintenance help supplied by most districts. Bus drivers have long been recognized as potential friends to children with learning problems. In the same way the building custodian or a cafeteria worker can sometimes be a substantial addition to the educational program of a building. Here a teacher must be sure that the guidelines for such help are made very explicit. In one school the principal agreed to let the custodian work with several boys one afternoon a week, showing them how to repair typewriters and thermostats. For the custodian this was a way to help pass along his expertise, for the district it was low-cost career education, for the teacher it was a time to work on class projects clearly beyond the abilities of these boys and to the boys it was the highlight of the week's activities!

BEWARE OF INCONSISTENT REINFORCEMENT!

The farther you get from self-contained organization, the more you will need consistent aid from all adults you enlist to help. With consistent reinforcement in operation in a program of behavior modification, it is possible to shape behavior along desired lines in the least possible amount of time. If a second team teacher follows your program for a child, it will be that much more successful.

> *Consistent reinforcement* is giving the same response to the same stimulus every time the behavior is emitted.

> *Inconsistent reinforcement* is an intermittent response pattern for the same stimulus.

A good illustration of inconsistent reinforcement is what happens when a substitute teacher comes to a classroom. The regular teacher has conditioned the class to expect certain procedures in certain sequences or at certain times; if the substitute doesn't keep to the same routine, she may be *reinforcing intermittently.* If the substitute differs markedly on procedures that are crucial for certain children with learning problems, she will find herself with some wild and disturbed children on her hands. By failing to supply the response these children have come to expect, she has blown their security to smithereens, and, temporarily, they may be worse off than if they had stayed at home that day.

To counteract the probability of inconsistent reinforcement by substitute teachers, schools should provide as much guidance as possible to those filling this role. If a booklet can be procured or written by district personnel, it could be given to all persons accepted for placement on the list of substitutes to be utilized during the coming year. Thus the substitutes would receive guidance at a time when they would be free to read helpful material. In addition, substitutes need guidance when they come to a specific building and a specific classroom.

USING THE SUBSTITUTE TEACHER TO BEST ADVANTAGE

Classroom teachers trying to individualize or carry on a behavior modification program often dread what will happen when a substitute teacher takes over for a day or two. At the same time, the substitute often leads the life of frustration personified, trying to carry out plans and activities outlined for the day, with little or no warning about special needs of children in the class.

Most children in most regular classrooms are able to adjust to the differences in behavior expectations, from regular teacher to substitute. But the fact that programs of behavior modification are built upon specific guidelines and expectations makes it imperative that these be made known to other adults working with the group. He or she may try his best to adapt to each classroom's personality, yet fail to provide the proper structure—the proper specific reinforcers—needed by certain children in the group.

Mr. Tota, a fourth grade classroom teacher, decided to make up some notes for substitute teachers who might be taking over his class during the year. He left these inside his plan book on his desk, since he knew that this was the first place substitutes in his building looked for help. Here is what the notes said:

Good morning! Welcome to a great group! I hope you have a satisfying day.

I do not expect you to carry out the plans in this book. It would be helpful if you could keep the same general time schedule as outlined here, since the children are conditioned to expect them; but I would feel badly to return and find out you had not felt free to share some of your talents and interests with my class. Artistic? Scientific? Nature lover? Math nut? Wonderful! Just ask the group where the various supplies are, and help yourself. Diane, Warren, Mark and Austin are reliable helpers.

There are packages of old Weekly Readers in the bottom file drawer and lots of ditto'd worksheets and unused games in the grey cupboard. Please use any of these you wish.

Note the following list of children in this group with special needs, physical and emotional.

Please be *sure* to leave notes on any problems encountered, especially with these boys and girls. I would also like to know exactly what you did with the class—page numbers or copies of worksheets used.

Thank you very much for sharing your day with us. I do not mind if you use my plans, as long as you understand what I want done; if not, please don't try to use them at all.

Sincerely,
Conrad Tota

Children with special needs:
June: Praise for any correct work, esp. math. Be casual about mistakes.
Eric: Commend if he works in his seat more than five minutes, if you notice this. *Try* to ignore him when he crawls under your desk, unless it is time to go to another class.
Esther: diabetic—note if she appears drowsy and call Nurse-Teacher's office.
Walter: Be sure he takes his medication at the Health Office just before lunch. (He often forgets.)

HOW CAN YOUR PRINCIPAL HELP?

A building principal has the unique potential for perceiving and using the totality of strengths exhibited by individual teachers in his building. No teacher can be a master in all areas; conversely, even the least experienced person on the staff has unique talents to contribute.

Ideally the principal serves as a catalyst, opening up communication among building personnel. The result should be a place where all teachers feel secure and respected in their respective areas of expertise. Here is a list compiled by a principal of our acquaintence; note that the talents listed include both cognitive (academic) and affective (psycho-social, non-academic) realms:

Teacher's Name	*Talent*
Phyllis	math manipulatives
Ron	designing inquiry packages
Dorothy	interpreting behavior of atypical children
Carol	listener, clarifier in staff groups
Jackie	personalized reading methods (intermediate)
Dave	behavior modification (spent two years working with disturbed children)

This list could be extended to include every faculty member. A good principal doesn't publish such a list or announce at staff meetings who is best at what, but *he should know.* And in knowing he should diplomatically pair or team teachers, either permanently or on an *ad hoc* basis. He should work to provide opportunities for such pairs of teachers to work together for their mutual growth. Some pairs may be chosen because the two share interests or talents; others may excel in different areas and complement one another.

Mrs. Baker, a second grade teacher skilled in creating reading materials, might be paired with Mr. Guglin, a fourth grade teacher who excels in inquiry approaches to social studies. This would be done to provide insight for Mrs. Baker into a new social studies text or curriculum based on the inquiry method. (A bonus for Mr. Guglin might be ideas for developing social studies materials for students reading below grade level. In many situations only one member will profit, at least immediately.)

Although most teachers have taken a great many college courses in education, experience has shown that their student-teaching experience, observation opportunities and in-service projects will provide the most important—most influential— training in their careers. Educational opportunities in a "job" situation under the supervision of the building principal can be the most effective teacher-training they receive. This type of supportive environment is almost completely dependent upon the principal's structuring and nurturing it.

Another way he can help is by encouraging any program of behavior modification being put into operation in the building. Having a teacher describe in a staff meeting what she did or is doing can help others to try some of the same techniques. He can also smooth out some of the difficulties which might be encountered by a teacher. It may be difficult for one teacher to tell another that he is reinforcing the wrong behavior in a child; often a skilled principal can find a way to communicate this without making the teacher approached become defensive. This is especially important if the matter concerns transferring a child out of a certain teacher's class. Teachers—conscientious ones— like to feel they can always meet the needs of all students, an unrealistic standard.

Principals have the authority to schedule in-service workshops and courses to help teachers learn more about behavioral techniques and their potential influence upon the instructional program. Many speakers and materials are available to explore further what programs of behavioral modification can do for a school.

Since they control the purse strings, principals should also allow an atmosphere where teachers feel free to order and use any kind of continuous progress materials which they can justify, within budgetary limits.

ENLIST YOUR PARENTS

Volunteers mentioned earlier in this chapter are usually parents of children in a teacher's class. But sometimes parents can be trained to carry on in the home setting a program of behavior modification you have begun in the classroom.

The procedure is the same as before: explain the guidelines and goals carefully. This is especially important in this situation since you will not be there to supervise the implementation of the program. It is wise to have the parent come in frequently for conferences if you try anything, to avoid inconsistent reinforcement or other such detrimental procedures. Often the parent is invited to observe the teacher in operation in the classroom before the parent begins his part; this is by far the best way to show him what the teacher wants him to do. Admittedly any program involving parents working with a child in the home is very difficult to administer, but occasionally there are parents able and willing to contribute to the growth of their children in this way.

SUMMARY

An awareness of all the adults associated with the school directly or indirectly can yield a rich harvest of help for the classroom teacher. The principal's role is crucial, for by his attitude he can support a program of behavior modification or cast doubt upon its value. He can build a network of support among his staff, widen their vision to include other adults available, inform them of local agencies for outside help and in many ways serve as the leader his role implies. A classroom teacher can do some of this but is limited if he does not have the support of his building principal.

13 CHANGES THAT LAST

In recent months, an educator friend was overheard describing the sampler she was going to have her mother embroider for her to hang near her desk at school. It would read:

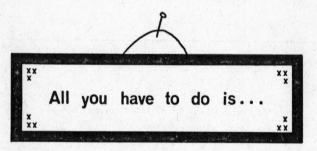

All you have to do is...

She said she was sick and tired of books and "visiting firemen" who give simplistic solutions for her most profound educational problems. We trust we have not implied in this book that changing the behavior of children from maladaptive to adaptive is always an easy thing to do. Indeed, sometimes it is comparatively uncomplicated when a teacher knows what techniques to use. But for a program of behavior modification to be both successful *and permanent,* it is important to observe a certain amount of professional caution.

A STEP AT A TIME

We have mentioned several times the need to proceed with great care. Frankly we know from personal experience how easy it is to gain enthusiasm for some new idea and start too many new things too quickly. *Your program should be only as large and as complex as your professional and personal skill to handle its ramifications.*

If, for example, you find yourself unable to use a hypertense parent as an ally, face this fact and proceed from there. In this particular illustration you might try one of the following alternatives:

1. Enlist the principal's help in counselling the parent.
2. Use another specialist, such as the school social worker.
3. Cut down on the amount of direct communication between yourself and that particular parent—at least temporarily.
4. Consciously cut down on your expectations for the amount of support you can expect from that parent.

Start using behavior modification (and perhaps you have already tried a few techniques) by working with one child. As you progress, start work with a second. Try to make changes that will take care of themselves; daily individual conferences or large amounts of teacher-made materials sound wonderful but swallow a discouraging amount of time. In short, preserve your own mental health!

OBSERVING BEHAVIOR AND RECORDING IT

Allow time along the way for constant evaluation and reevaluation of your programs and techniques. *Remember, the child's behavior will tell you what you need to know.* Train yourself to be observant. In this sense every class is an opportunity to evaluate the progress of your students.

To plan and evaluate programs of behavior modification, properly prepared anecdotal records are a must. Knowing how to observe a child and how to record that observation is a skill highly worthy of development. Then can you use that concrete record to draw subjective conclusions concerning a child's adjustment and learning patterns.

The atmosphere in which you observe is crucial. You will be changing your role from instructor and helper to that of diagnostic observer. The younger the children the more difficult this is to accomplish. Of course if you have an open classroom or a full-time aide, you can simply arrange for someone else to teach a lesson in whatever subject seems to be causing problems. Then you can sit back in a corner and observe. The next best situation is to observe the child in a special area, such as music or physical education. Even though this may be in a different physical surrounding from your classroom, the teacher will be someone familiar to the child. Lunchtime could be another opportunity to observe, although you ought to remember that behaviors you observe may be quite different patterns from what you usually see in your classroom. (More about this later.) The important thing to remember is that the class must be under the *control* of someone else. For this reason it is best to avoid observing too early in the day; children might be confused by your changed role.

Set a definite time limit for your observation. Even five minutes' observation with the principal teaching the class can be a revelation. But the time period should be recorded for proper interpretation of the observation record.

The procedure itself requires no particular training; simply jot down as fast as you can *every behavior* you see the child do. We like listing by phrases. Do not stop to evaluate whether or not a certain behavior is significant—write it down and decide later. Your anecdotal record might look something like this:

Record for observing _Kay Juraios_

Date _10/7/75_ Activity_____

Observer _Mrs. Donoghue_

Time period _15 Min_

picks up pencil
prints first name on paper

```
looks at teacher, with
reading group
chews on eraser
looks out the window (noise)
slowly pushes paper off desk
looks at teacher to see if
    she noticed (she didn't)
picks up the paper
copies one word from board
picks her nose
watches Judy talk to Jane
notices teacher looking
    at her
copies 2 more words
plays with pencil
breaks point
```

Note that this observer has not tried to analyze the child's motives or pass judgment upon what she has done; all she is doing is recording the actual behaviors, placing any other environmental influences in parentheses. But note also how clearly this child has communicated to the observer by her actions that she is not interested or is not capable of copying the words from the chalkboard. Sometimes it is useful to do the first observation on a child who has what you consider good patterns of learning behavior. Then when you observe a child with problems you will have another child with whom to compare him.

Interpreting the anecdotal record is important, for this is the purpose of the whole activity. If you have observed a child while someone with similar teaching style is in charge of the group, you will doubtless find the experience even more useful. Usually by examining an anecdotal record—or even while recording it—you can note the similarity of the child's behavior patterns to those you usually see when *you* are teaching. But be careful to use all of your observation time to write your anecdotal notes; do not try to judge such things. You can do that later from your anecdotal record.

There is an advantage to observing a child in a totally different setting, especially if you have problems with him and the other teacher does not. Perhaps it would be possible to observe the child in several different settings to see how he reacts to various teachers behaviorally.

To point out the superior usefulness of objective observations, here are two accounts of the same behaviors:

Poor anecdotal record	*Good anecdotal record*
wastes time	looks at ceiling
gets angry	purses lips
	slams book on desk
does his work	Completes on page
annoys others	takes Paul's pen
	laughs
	puts pen in desk

Note that in the good record there is no attempt to evaluate motives or even to evaluate the actions themselves. The purpose of observing a child and recording his behaviors in an anecdotal record is to clarify to yourself just what his behaviors and behavior patterns are. You may think that Gus wastes a lot of time, but this is really your subjective judgment, your opinion; if you were to observe that in five minutes he copied a total of three words from the chalkboard, this is objective observation.

Sometimes a carefully recorded observation can correct a wrong impression. Mrs. Pitts was an experienced fourth grade teacher. While working with reading groups she noticed out of the corner of her eye that Warren was not doing his seatwork assignment. The next day she noticed the same thing. When it happened a third time, she decided she had better check on the situation. When the group met the next day she watched Warren carefully, for wasting time was not his usual pattern. What she discovered made her glad she had not scolded him prematurely: he had done several pages of independent work on his project, he had read fifteen to twenty pages in his assigned book, and he was really listening to her reading group discuss the story because it concerned horses, one of his special interests. What a wise teacher to allow time for eyes to rest a minute and for a mind to follow an interest.

USING RECORDS

Many times there are cumulative records concerning a certain child that would save a teacher a great deal of time and give her much needed information for planning the most appropriate program of behavior modification. Permanent records of several varieties are usually on file: medical records in the health office, standardized folders with test scores and anecdotal records in the school office, and sometimes some kind of folder or packet which goes with the child from one teacher to the next.

Health records are of primary importance. If a child cannot hear or see, he will have difficulty learning in a regular classroom, unless the program is adapted in some way. If he needs and has glasses but does not bother to wear them, his school work is bound to suffer. If he is extremely anemic or hyperglycemic, he cannot be faulted for failing to achieve up to potential, no matter how innovative an instructional program he is exposed to. There is no way a teacher can modify a child's behavior if a physical limit to his activity exists. These are reasons why the School Nurse-Teacher ought to be involved in any team effort to deal with behavior problems.

The quality of all school records depends largely upon the building principal, but especially so with permanent record folders. Although many school districts determine in general what does and does not belong in a child's folder, the principal can do much to improve the usefulness of information recorded there. Teachers should be instructed in how to write truly anecdotal records, rather than teacher judgments. They should also be required to file complete test copies, rather than just cover sheets, since complete tests often reveal error patterns not readily detectable in score sheets. There should be some kind of notation on each permanent record folder concerning any specialized testing or report filed elsewhere. And even in a completely ungraded situation there should be clear record of the grade level in which the child is considered: we have personally encountered several situations where it took some doing to unravel transfer records and also to determine which form of a test to use so that the proper norms would apply.

In many schools it is customary to eliminate certain test scores several years later "when they become outdated." Reading readiness tests often fall into this category. While it is true that children change, and thick folders take more file space, it seems a shame to dispose of information which is sometimes invaluable in tracing the history of learning difficulties. In our opinion it is a good use of file space to retain such information, especially reading readiness tests, even into junior high and high school. This is especially valid for children with whom there seems to be some question of ability or achievement.

USING OUTSIDE AGENCIES

Any professional educator should be able to recognize a situation where there are too many problems for him to solve alone. We did not feel it was appropriate to mention this at the beginning of the book, for fear many would use this as an excuse for not trying behavior modification; but we do feel it is only realistic to admit that for various reasons some problems are beyond solving in the school setting. There are limits to the number of children with extreme behavior problems of differing types one teacher can cope with at once. Teachers have physical limits, and if their energies are required for constant adjustment to new programs, they cannot be expected to fill up twenty-four hours a day with professional reading and consultation on problems not before encountered. Furthermore, if the building principal does not support a teacher's attempts at solving problems revealed through maladaptive behavior, there is a definite limit to how much an individual teacher can accomplish on his own.

Many problems commonly recognized as being beyond the scope of the regular classroom can be solved through the use of behavior modification as outlined in this book; still others can be solved through the use of community agencies of all kinds. We mentioned in Chapter 12 the need for the building principal to be sure teachers are informed as to the community resources available to them. When teachers know the resources at hand for extreme behavior problems, they may be encouraged to use personnel from those agencies as school resources and also to deal with problems they know would not qualify for special programs.

DEAL WITH YOUR FEELINGS

If you wish to avoid the most common pitfall, deal honestly with your own emotional involvement in your programs of behavior modification. Many programs have been abandoned prematurely because a teacher began a program he was unable to continue on a long-term basis; others were continued long after they were really needed.

As an illustration, suppose you have in your class a child with behavior problems. And suppose that this child has some characteristic that offends you deeply. To a great extent your maturity and professional background should enable you to overcome such a prejudice and seek to help this child as diligently as you would any other. But sometimes this kind of situation reaches a point where the child and the teacher would both be better off if the child were transferred to another classroom, even during the school year. At such a juncture it takes a mature professional to admit that he has reached his limit. Again it is the building principal who must establish an atmosphere where such a situation would be faced honestly for the good of the child.

Professional pride is also a hindrance when temporary discouragement causes a teacher to give up a program of behavior modification because fellow teachers question its wisdom. Teachers need the courage of their convictions. Try to find at least one professional somewhere who has the same concern for establishing such programs; this ally might be a teacher in your building or a neighbor who teaches in a school across town. Sharing insights and programs can multiply your efforts many times over.

USING RESOURCE ROOMS FOR BEHAVIORAL PROGRAMS

Teachers interested in developing supportive programs should study the many different approaches now being tried in other schools for meeting specific needs. These can often be used to provide the type of programs and materials recommended for techniques of behavior modification. Reading labs, for example, may be useful for the consistent and positive reinforcement so important in a behavioral program, provided the child's prescription is based upon his instructional baseline; that is, provided it includes a recognition of the child's non-academic baseline in forming his work assignments.

Adjunct centers, resource centers, resource rooms and other such areas should follow principles of good behavior modification in keeping the emphasis positive; dwelling on *weaknesses only* will tend to stress the negative and become self-defeating.

Sometimes one teacher on a team will find he most enjoys dealing with children who need the structure and encouragement of behavior modification programs in a special way; his fellow professionals would do well to recognize this and use him as a resource. Perhaps this might involve his teaching a building in-service session or a reassignment of team teachers, so that this particular teacher could have a smaller number of specially selected children, chosen with his talents in mind.

WHATEVER WORKS IS WONDERFUL!

Throughout these pages we have described many basic principles considered necessary if a teacher is to change a child's behavior. We have also suggested many ways in which a teacher can put these ideas into practice. We have sought to be dogmatic only when we felt it essential, otherwise we were flexible.

The one final measure of success is whether or not "it works." Did you solve your problem? Did you change the child's maladaptive behavior patterns? You may have used some technique exactly as we described it, or you may have adapted it. Great! Whatever works is wonderful!

Have we changed your behavior as a teacher? We hope so—sincerely we do. That was our goal in presenting this book. May you use it to find new ways of teaching more effectively, so that children may learn.

INDEX

205

Defeated child: *(cont.)*
  program for inability to write, 158-159
  radical change in total achievement, 154
  raising expectancies, 162
  rarely aggressive or withdrawn, 150
  readiness, 154
  reinforcements, 161
  remedial program, 152, 155
  report cards, 154
  reports of parent-teacher conferences, 154
  sample papers, 154
  sensitive, 153
  set own goals and timetables, 160, 161
  setting objectives, 159
  shaping, 161, 162
  shows on historical and geographical topics, 160
  slide-taking, 159, 160
  spelling and writing, 152
  subskills, 155
  success in areas of weakness, 156
  success too much to tolerate, 154
  tape-recorded narrative, 159
  teacher appraisals, 154
  teacher as consultant, 160
  timetable deadlines, 159
  unequally developed abilities, 152, 153, 154
Denial, 143
Desensitization, 172
Destructiveness:
  disruptive child, 121-134
  quiet child, 138
Differences, individual, 24
Difficulty level, 91
Direction, 82
Directive teaching, 27
Discipline, misuse of word, 130
Disruptive child:
  appears strong and self-controlled, 126
  background, 124
  case, 125-126
  continue program, 129
  control situation, 129

Disruptive child *(cont.)*
  dealing with personal frustrations, 133
  decide what offensive behavior is, 128-129
  defining disruptive behavior, 123-124
  development of pattern, 124
  distracting classmates, 123
  education contributes to upset, 124
  emotional stimulation, 124
  encourage adaptive behavior, 127-128
  fear, 126
  forced apologies, 131
  ignore negative behavior, 128
  institutionalized for life, 123
  instructional baselines, 129
  interfere with program, 123
  interrupting group work, 123
  isolating and labelling, 123
  keeping own progress chart, 129
  living in disruptive world, 124
  missing directions, 123
  misuse of word "discipline," 130
  needs, 126-127
    control over inner destructiveness, 127
    limits, 127
    models to follow, 127
    recognition for successes, 127
    repeated, explicit instructions, 127
    separate emotion from behavior, 127
    situation under control, 126
  overstimulating group, 133
  pay for damage, 131
  procedure, 128-129
  psychological evaluation and help, 123
  punching people, 123
  regular praise, 129
  scuttle learning atmosphere, 124
  "socially-disruptive," 123
  special class placement, 123
  stop reinforcing offensive behavior, 129
  symptom substitution, 130
  tense atmosphere, 124
  testing, 123